Buddhist Tantra
and
Buddhist Art

Emerging Perceptions in Buddhist Studies

(ISSN 0971-9512)

1-2. An Encyclopaedia of Buddhist Deities, Demigods, Godlings, Saints & Demons — with Special Focus on Iconographic Attributes; by Fredrick W. Bunce. 2 Vols. (ISBN 978-81-246-0020-7; set)

3. Buddhism in Karnataka; by R.C. Hiremath; with a foreword by H.H. the Dalai Lama (ISBN 978-81-246-0013-9)

4-5. Pāli Language and Literature: A Systematic Survey and Historical Study; by Kanai Lal Hazra. 2 Vols. (ISBN 978-81-246-0004-7; set)

6. Maṇḍala and Landscape; by A.W. Macdonald (ISBN 978-81-246-0060-3)

7. The Future Buddha Maitreya: An Iconological Study; by Inchang Kim (ISBN 978-81-246-0082-5)

8. Absence of the Buddha Image in Early Buddhist Art; by Kanoko Tanaka (ISBN 978-81-246-0090-0)

9. A Few Facts About Buddhism; by Gunnar Gällmo (ISBN 978-81-246-0099-3)

10. Buddhist Theory of Meaning and Literary Analysis; by Rajnish K. Mishra (ISBN 978-81-246-0118-1)

11. Buddhism as/in Performance; Analysis of Meditation and Theatrical Practice; by David E.R. George (ISBN 978-81-246-0123-5)

13. Buddhist Art in India and Sri Lanka: 3rd Century BC to 6th Century AD — A Critical Study; by Virender Kumar Dabral (ISBN 978-81-246-0162-4)

14. The Tibetan Iconography of Buddhas, Bodhisattvas and Other Deities: A Unique Pantheon; by Lokesh Chandra & Fredrick W. Bunce (ISBN 978-81-246-0178-5)

15. The Dalai Lamas: The Institution and Its History by Ardy Verhaegen; (ISBN 978-81-246-0202-7)

16. The Tibetan Tāntric Vision; by Krishna Ghosh Della Santina (ISBN 978-81-246-0227-0)

17. The Buddhist Art of Kauśāmbī: From 300 BC to AD 550; by Aruna Tripathi (ISBN 978-81-246-0226-3)

18. Mahāmudrā & Atiyoga; by Giuseppe Baroetto; Translated from Italian into English by Andrew Lukianowicz (ISBN 978-81-246-0322-2)

19. Theravāda Buddhist Devotionalism in Ceylon, Burma and Thailand; by V.V.S. Saibaba (ISBN 978-81-246-0327-7)

20. Faith and Devotion in Theravāda Buddhism; by V.V.S. Saibaba (ISBN 978-81-246-0329-1)

21. Sects in Tibetan Buddhism: Comparison of Practices Between Gelugpa and Nyingmapa Sects; by Vijay Kumar Singh (ISBN 978-81-246-0330-7)

22. Emptiness and Becoming: Integrating Mādhyamika Buddhism and Process Philosophy; by Peter Paul Kakol (ISBN 978-81-246-0519-6)

23. Buddhist Ethics in Impermanence; by M.V. Ram Kumar Ratnam, K. Srinivas (ISBN 978-81-246-0562-2)

Emerging Perceptions in Buddhist Studies, no. 12

Buddhist Tantra and Buddhist Art

T.N. Mishra

DK PRINTWORLD
Publishers of Indian Traditions

Cataloging in Publication Data — DK
[Courtesy: D.K. Agencies (P) Ltd. <docinfo@dkagencies.com>]

Mishra T.N., (Tej Narain), 1945-
Buddhist tantra and Buddhist art.
(Emerging perceptions in Buddhist studies, no. 12).
Includes bibliographical references (p.).
Includes index.
ISBN 13: 9788124601419

1. Tantric Buddhism. 2. Art, Buddhist. 3. Buddhism.
4. Philosophy, Buddhist. I. Title. II. Series: Emerging perceptions in Buddhist studies; no. 12.

ISBN 13: 978-81-246-0141-9
First edition published in 2000
Second impression, 2014

Printed and published by :
D.K. Printworld (P) Ltd.
Regd. office : *Vedaśrī*, F-395, Sudarshan Park
(Metro Station: Ramesh Nagar)
New Delhi - 110 015
Phones : (011) 2545 3975, 2546 6019; *Fax*: (011) 2546 5926
e-mail : indology@dkprintworld.com
Web : www.dkprintworld.com

Acknowledgements

FOR the collection of relevant materials for this volume, I am indebted to many scholars and institutions, of these, mention may particularly be made of those scholars whose published books and articles were consulted during the preparation of this volume, and others who supplied me unpublished information during discussion that contributed to the formation of my ideas. I am very much indebted to my spiritual teacher for his help and guidance over a decade; I am equally grateful to other *ācāryas*, saints, and monks for their guidance and suggestions.

I am very much indebted to *ācārya* Pandit Brahma Gopal Bhaduri, for his kind help, guidance, and useful dialogues. I am equally grateful for the help, answer to certain quaries, and suggestions of Dr. Miss Krishna Banerjee, Reader, Department of English (M.M.V.) and Dr. T.K. Biswas, Joint Director, Bharat Kala Bhavan, Banaras Hindu University who has gone through the manuscript and made valuable suggestions. I am obliged to Dr. Deena Bandhu Pandey, Head of the Depatment of History of Art, Banaras Hindu University and all my colleague of Bharat Kala Bhavan, B.H.U., who time to time gave encouragements in the preparation of this book.

My thanks are also due to Bharat Kala Bhavan Library, Philosophy Depatment Library, Central Library of B.H.U., Saraswati Pustakalaya, Sampurnanand Sanskrit Visvavidyalaya (Varanasi), and some personal libraries.

I also wish to mention here the moral support I received from my wife Vandana and my daughters Kavita, Pratima, and Jyoti in course of preparation of this work.

T.N. Mishra

Contents

List of Illustrations

(*prajñā*) is Nairātmyā and with her *śakti* he is known to have left his impact on a number of god concepts in Vajrayāna Buddhism. It is said that *śūnya* personified takes the shape of Heruka when male and that of Nairātmya when female, when in deep embrace with his *prajñā* or *śakti* (*yuganaddha*, *yāb-yum*) or number of forms of which Hevajra is the most important.

Fig. 8: Hevajra (metal), Bharat Kala Bhavan.

Fig. 9: Prajñāpāramitā (stone) — Probably thirteenth century AD from Candi Sari temple, Java (Indonesia), stone.

Prajñāpāramitā is the embodiment of the *pāramitā-sūtra* and she is considered to be the goddess of transcendental knowledge which *sūtra* stands for. Her worship is very popular among the Buddhist devotee who would like to gain this supreme knowledge.

Fig. 10: Prajñāpāramitā (metal), Bharat Kala Bhavan.

Fig. 11: Tārā (metal), Bharat Kala Bhavan — Tārā occupies the same position in Buddhist pantheon as the great goddess Durgā does in the Hindu. The religious belief in the feminine principle as an active force in the universe finds recognition in the fullest measure. And considered to be the personified energy (*śakti*) of her consort and to have manifested herself in innumerable forms. Tārā is described to be the consort of *dhyānī* Buddha, Amoghasiddhi. She is also believed to be the consort of Avalokiteśvara, the *bodhisattva* of great compassion by whom she is said to have been charged with the alleviation of the miseries of all beings. Apart from such associations, which endow her with a dual personality, she occupies the position of the supreme goddess in Buddhism of Mahāyāna and Vajrayāna affiliations. The word *tārā* (*tāriṇī*), by which name this great goddess is known, seems to have been derived from the root *tār*, i.e., to cross. In this sense the worship of the goddess is said to help the devotee to cross the ocean of existence. Another meaning of root *tār* is to save as 'protect' and as such Tārā is also recognised to be the saviour goddess protecting her worshippers from all the evil of existence.

Fig. 12: Avalokiteśvara (metal), Bharat Kala Bhavan — Avalokiteśvara is the most popular god in the Buddhist pantheon. He is the second *bodhisattva* in the Buddhist scriptures after Mañjuśrī. *Bodhisattva* Avalokiteśvara is said to have emanated from *dhyānī* Buddha and to be ruling divinity during the present *kalpa* which start from disappearance of Gautama Buddha and is to end with the advent of Maitreya in future Buddha. The most important aspect of his conception is reflected in the belief that he refused *nirvāṇa* until all created beings should attain the supreme knowledge (*anuttara-jñāna*). This Mahāyāna attitude made him the most popular among the Buddhists and for this he is considered to be the Lord of infinite compassion (*parama-kāruṇika*) and mercy, embodying, in a manner, the teaching of the Master.

Fig. 13: Amitāyuṣa (metal), Bharat Kala Bhavan.

Fig. 14: The Maṇḍala of Heruka, Thangaka, in private collection.

Fig. 15: *Bodhisattva*, second century AD, Bharat Kala Bhavan (Stone).

Fig. 16: Mañjuśrī (teracotta) 18th century AD, Bharat Kala Bhavan.

Introduction

TWENTY-FIVE hundred years ago India witnessed an intellectual and religious revolution which culminated in the overthrow of monotheism, priestly selfishness, and the establishment of a synthetic religion, a system of light and thought which was appropriately called *dhamma* of Buddha. The beauty of Buddhism is that it is a well-regulated and scientific way of life, and not a religion in its narrow sense of spiritualism with dogma and rituals. The Master (Buddha) gave simple and scientific ways for peace, happiness, and *nirvāṇa* — All this is possible through *bhāvanā*.

The word *bhāvanā*, used repeatedly in Buddhist scriptures, is a Pāli word, and it means culture on mental development. It aims at cleansing mind of impurities and mental disturbances such as lustful desires, hatred, ill-will, indolence, worries, and restlessness. It aims at cultivating qualities like concentration, awareness, intelligence, will, and tranquillity. This mental development ultimately leads one to the attainment of the highest wisdom which would help us in the understanding of nature of things as they are. Buddha gave the world Four Noble Truths — "suffering, origin of suffering, cessation of suffering, and the way to cessation." This, coupled with his Eightfold Path, are key to the success and satiation in this life. Compassion, right action, right livelihood, right efforts, and good intentions are the key words around which Buddhism revolves.

Throughout the history of Indian civilisation, there has been a certain inspiring ideal, a certain motive power, a certain way of looking at life, which cannot be identified with any one stage of the process. Hinduism has grown not by accretion, but like an organism, undergoing, from time to time, transformations as a whole. It has carried within it much of its early attributes. It is the historic vitality and the abounding energy that, it reveals, helped to sustain its spiritual genius throughout. The unity of Hinduism is not one of an unchanging creed, neither it is a fixed deposit of doctrines, but it evinces a sort of unity of a continuously changing life. Religion is thus an experience and an attitude of the mind, a consciousness about the ultimate reality and is not a theory about the God. The aim of all religions is the realisation of the highest truth. It is the intuition of reality, the insight into truth, contact with the supreme, that form the basic elements of Hindu philosophy. Worship is the acknowledgement of the magnificence of this Supreme Reality. From the beginning, attempts have been made to bring the Supreme Being closer to the needs of man.

The Indian philosophical tradition has been a quest, both for an immediate experience of reality and for an achievement of the good and just life. Men and society have been nourished in India not by ethical and social, but by mystical and trans-social doctrines and ideals. Metaphysics thus becomes the law of man's social living. The Indian ethical system is built on the foundation of metaphysics, certain doctrines, and symbols, and all these invest morality with rich, trans-human meanings. Metaphysics and religion both impart superhuman meanings to the evolutionary process and encourage mankind to evaluate, order, and direct it as frequently as it suffers defeat at the hand of nature. Whosoever feels a universal love for his fellow creatures will rejoice in conferring bliss on them, and thus attaining *nirvāṇa* on the bliss of his apprehension of non-duality, he overcomes ignorance and sorrow, secures peace, and never suffers degradation. Man reaches his highest moral status when his feeling, joy, and reverence reflect themselves in his relations to the external world through a more sensitive and universalised conscience in terms of a complete acceptance, peace, and an all-transcending compassion or love. Ill-feeling or hatred is essentially self-destructive. Inner calm and altruism, which constitute one level of spiritualism, is good for your own well-being. If you create pain for others, you will suffer and will harm your peace of mind, such is the indispensable contribution of the mystical consciousness to the elevation of moral standards through the discipline of human nature for progress.

In India, a highly well developed civilisation had been flourishing for centuries. Its religious life, in the period between 750 BC-320 BC displayed certain characteristic features. The first and foremost being the introduction of the images of gods, as worship and meditation of the Supreme Being was thought possible only when He was endowed with a form. There was the belief that the form of the Supreme Being, as He manifests Himself, should be worshipped according to the rites prescribed. The Vedas were considered as the infallible source of spiritual truth, and the rituals prescribed therein, were considered as the sole means of salvation or emancipation. The essential elements common between the two theistic religions, viz., Śaivism and Vaiṣṇavism, are *bhakti* (devotion) and *prasāda* (divine grace). *Bhakti* means intense love and devotion of the worshipper to his beloved god, even to the extent of complete self-surrender. The *prasāda* means the grace of god which brings salvation to the devotee.

This period was lit up on the other hand by the personality of two great reformers, Mahāvīra and Gautama Buddha. They were wandering ascetics who ignored god and denied the Vedas, and revolted against the superiority of the brāhmaṇas. There were other people also who criticised the Vedic religion and discarded the Vedas completely and openly. One such person was Cārvāka. But the more powerful, systematic, and philosophic challenges were posed by the founders of Jainism and Buddhism. Sāṁkhya and Upaniṣad served the sources of their inspiration; the gospel of freedom from misery and even the theory of *karma* (action) were borrowed by them from contemporary religious thought and were systematised by them. Jainism and Buddhism had shared certain common elements philosophically; they both started from the same fundamental principle that the world is full of misery, and the object of religion is to find means of deliverance from the endless cycle of births and deaths which bring men repeatedly into this world. As *karma* (action) or an individual action is the root cause of rebirth, emphasis was laid upon conduct and the practice of austerities in varying degrees of severity as the chief means of salvation; and therefore they went against the sacrifice and remained indifferent to prayers to the personal God. Jainism and Buddhism both went for a system of philosophy and social organisation, with a code of morality and cult of their own, which together gave to their followers a sense of religious solidarity.

In the very beginning of early Buddhism, and even when Mahāyānism sprang up, a strict discipline was enjoined on the followers of the faith. The rules were indeed very good and attractive at the time of the Buddha but served the purpose only for a certain time but not always. Buddha did not permit the consumption of fish, meat, wine, and association with opposite sex in the church, among other things. The result was that even during the lifetime of the Buddha, many monks are said to have revolted against his injunctions; there were many others who did not openly revolt against the Buddha's injunctions but, nevertheless, violated them in secret. The result was that there arose secret conclaves of Buddhists who, though professing to be monks, violated all rules of morality and discipline and secretly practised what was disapproved by the Buddha and his followers, and disallowed in practice. After the death of the Buddha, such secret conclaves must have grown in numbers, till they formed a school of thought in themselves.

The secret Buddhist conclaves that grew on the ruins of the monastic order developed, in course of time, into big organisations known as Guhyasamāja which held their teachings and practices in secret (*guhya*). Thus, the *Guhya-samāja-tantra* was composed in the *saṁgīti* form (collection of verses). It explained why the teachings of the school were kept secret for so long, and now even a devout Buddhist could practise all that was enjoined in the Tantra, together with details of theories and practices with rituals. Its most important declaration was that the emancipation does not depend on bodily sufferings and abstinence from all worldly enjoyments. The work lays down that perfection cannot be obtained through the satisfaction of all desires. Its teaching in this respect is direct and unequivocal.

The earlier concept of Buddhism lost itself significantly in the maze of Tāntric mysticism in it, and it was practically overwhelmed by the introduction of a host of *mudrā*s, *maṇḍala*s, *kriyā*s, and *caryā*s. Buddhism now began to incorporate elements like magical spells, exorcism, recognition of demons, and female deities (Śakti), and at the same time, *yoga* and sexo-*yogic* practices were entertained. All these resulted a significant change and what emerged came to be called Tāntric Buddhism. The influence of the Tāntric religion and philosophy is found recorded in the religious texts. Texts like *Mañjuśrīmūlakapa*, *Saddharmapuṇḍarīka*, *Prajñāpāramitā*, *Sādhanamālā*, *Niṣpanna Yogāvalī*, and some other texts incorporated different notions and rituals of Tantra in the Buddhist religion, philosophy, and iconography. The philosophy and religion of Tantra was thus formulated, and incourse of time, it made a tremendous impact on the religions. The impact of Tāntric tenets also seeped into the paintings and sculptural art of India.

The introduction of Tantrism affected a radical change in the outlook and character of Indian religion. The high ideals of religion, which aimed at the salvation of all and by the spirit of universal love for all mankind, yielded to gross superstitions and immoral practices so far as the general masses were concerned. Esoteric practices as the easiest means of attaining salvation retarted the growth of spiritual ideas, while the conception of ultimate reality as an embodiment of duality of male and female energy, paved the way for erotic and sensual practices including the undermining of the sense of moral values. The way advised for salvation was very dangerous for common people; most of them could not succeed and perished on the way. The rational and highly ethical teachings of Buddha were, thus, smoothered under a load of gross superstitions, ritualistic worship of host of deities, and an immoral life against each of which Buddha led a ceaseless crusade.

From the twelfth century onward there was a marked decline in religious practices as also in the field of art. The period from AD 1000 to 1300 was the period of transition, and marked the beginning of the Muslim dominance in India. By the close of this century almost all the important centres of northern Indian Buddhism were affected by Muslim invasions and there began a period of rapid decline. All the communities of India, had to face the disastrous and destructive inroads of Islam which were fired with the fanatic zeal including the demolishing of idols and temples; the intrusion of Islam brought an important change in the religious outlook of India as it introduced for the first time the generic name Hindu. So far Tāntric Buddhism was concerned, it turned into a religion of minority some of whom either continued their religious activities secretly while others fled to Nepal or Tibet for the security of their lives and continued their religious activities in an alien atmosphere.

India, the birth-place of Buddhism could not sustain the religion. Buddhism for its esoteric nature lost its touch with lay followers of grassroot level and the final *coup de etat* was brought into being by Islamic invasions.

1

Religion and Philosophy

IN FACT, each system claimed that it was the most coherent and the most comprehensive from the intellectual point of view. One might begin the speculative life in any tradition and in any realisation, but in between the two lay the realm of *manana*, logical thinking, without which faith becomes a superstition and realisation a make-believe. The literature of Indian philosophy is a vast one, testifying at once to the virility of thought and the keenness of feeling, that, what cannot be rationally justified has no right to intellectual allegiance.

The attempt of the human mind to account for the various forces and phenomena of nature with which man is confronted leads to rise of myths. When imagination interprets nature as the action of a personified being resembling a human agent, a myth is formed. The primitive phase of religious beliefs, the process of personification, makes gradual progress and natural phenomena develop into gods. The evaluation of religion and philosophical thought may begin with Vedic age, as it has preserved an aspect of primitive religious ideas. Although, R̥gvedic mythology is not as primitive as some scholars once believed it to be, in no other literary monuments of the world do we come across this primitive phase of the evolution of religious beliefs which reveals to us the very process of personification by which natural phenomena came to be conceived as Gods. The name of the god often hides but little.

The evolution of religion and philosophical thought in the post Ṛgvedic age begins with the *Atharvaveda* which has preserved an aspect of the primitive religious ideas which are not to be found in other Vedic tracts. It must be admitted that *Atharvaveda* religion, being more popular than priestly, formed a transitional stage to the idolatries and superstitions of the ignorant masses, rather than to the sublimated pantheism of the Upaniṣad, and further that it had magic confused with mysticism. Magic and religion are never confused in the Vedic religion. Original or otherwise, profound philosophical ideas cropped up now and then in *Atharvaveda*. In the said Veda, the *kāla* (time) as the first cause of all existence (XIX.53.56) is truly philosophical notion, but around it are woven metaphors that give a mystic twin to the great idea (XII.53). Similarly *prāṇa* (breath) and *kāma* (desire or love) are described as first cause (XI.4 and IX.2 respectively).

In Indian religion there must be a common element that makes every stage and every movement an expression of the concept of religion in its totality. The religion, in the form of literary records that have come down to us, is that of Indians. The simple hymns of the Veda reveal to us an age, when the tree in the jungle could speak and the river water could sing and man could listen and understand. Truth is found in every religion though in different measures. A man's religion is something integral to his nature. Whatever form of worship is taken up by individual faith, it is exalted into the highest. The greatest gift of life is the dream of a life. There are systems of thought, like Sāṁkhya and the Mīmāṁsā which cultivate a spirit and attitude to which it would be difficult to deny the name of religion, even though they may not accept any belief in god or gods superior to oneself. The Buddhists adopt other methods for achieving salvation from sin. It is the spirit in man that is responding to the spirit in the universe; the high vision of those who have penetrated into the depth of being, their sense of the divine in all their exaltation of feeling and enrichment of personality, have been the source of the noblest of works in the world.

In fact, what is final, is the religious experience itself, though its expressions change if they are to be relevant to the growing content of knowledge. The experience is what is felt by the individual in his deepest being, what is seen or heard by him, and this is valid for all times. The Vedic *ṛṣis* were the first who burst into that silent sea of the ultimate being and their utterances are found registered in ancient literature. The relation between the vision and its expression, the fact, and its interpretation, are very close. On the fundamental, metaphysical, and religious issues, different commentators offer different interpretations. The *Muṇḍaka Upaniṣad* says:

> the liberated soul enters into the all. The heart is released from its burden of care. The sorrows and errors of the past, the anxiety of unsatisfied desire, and suddenness of resentment are no more.
>
> — III.2.15

Transmigration means the flow of life beyond the cycle of birth and death. If *Brahman* is the eternal reality and if we are non-different from it, birth cannot be our beginning, nor death our end. The soul is eternal, though it appears to be born and to die. Birth and death relate to the integration and disintegration respectively of the elements that compose the physical body. These are changes that affect the body, like growth and decay. It is because the soul identified itself with the body, on account of ignorance, that it suffers and becomes a victim of *saṁsāra*. The kind of birth the soul takes and the type of enjoyment that falls to its lot are determined by its own past. The term *karma* means work and the result of work. And the law of *karma* simply states that the sphere of morality in an ordered realm, is the moral equivalent of the physical law of causality. Our present has issued out of our past, and our future will be defined on our present. *Mokṣa* (release) is the final goal of man. According to the doctrine of non-duality, one needs not wait till the dicease of the body for the attainment of release. *Mokṣa* is the eternal nature of the self. What prevents the soul from realising it is its own ignorance (*ajñāna*). When ignorance is dispelled through wisdom of the nature of self, one attains release. This is known as *jīvana-mukti*.[1]

The theory of emancipation requires that every individual should undergo a series of births and rebirths till his soul or consciousness is free from all impurities. Emancipation means cessation of births and rebirths, and therefore, of worldly miseries, which man, up to the present day, strove and still strives hard to attain. To the average Indian, the present life is a misery and devoid of all interests. He cares more for an improved condition in the next birth than his material prosperity in this.

Every individual has a physical and mental side. Our exepriences are dependent on both; while material facilities could fulfil one's physical needs, only spirituality could ease a man's mental agony. Today great efforts are being made to acquire material facilities; though these are important, human beings should not forget the spiritual aspect. Ill-feeling or hatred essentially leads to self-destruction. Inner calm and altruism, which constitute one's level of spirituality, is good for one's own well-being. If you create pain for others, you will suffer, and it will harm your own peace of mind.

Any religion of the world could be good or the best religion for one, but not for everybody. One religion cannot satisfy all varieties of people. While at the individual level, one religion and one truth may be all important, yet at the community level there will be several religions and several truths. So, religious pluralism is relevant. The concept at one religion and one truth is very important for an individual to develop faith. It is hypocrisy to say that all religions are the same. Different religions constitute different approaches altogether. If a man has no firm faith in his religion, he cannot put his heart and soul into its practice. Religion has always given a message of peace and co-existence.

Twenty-five hundred years ago India witnessed an intellectual and religious revolution which culminated in the overthrow of monotheism, priestly selfishness, and the establishment of a synthetic religion, a

---

1. *Chāndogya Upaniṣad* (VIII.13-15); *Taittirīya Upaniṣad* (Brahmānananda-vallī); *Muṇḍaka Upaniṣad* (III.13); *Bhagavad Gītā* (VII.16-17).

system of light and thought which was called *dhamma* (philosophical religion). The Buddha uses terms of great significance — they are 'sight' and 'insight'. 'Sight' with 'insight' is wisdom. It is the bridge that conducts one's life to the ultimate truth. The Buddha says that the main, if not the only, means to get 'insight' is through meditation. In a destructive world, meditation alone gives us that wisdom which lends purpose to our activities and provide direction to our physical and metaphysical quests.

The beauty of Buddhism is that it is a well-regulated and scientific way of life, and not a religion in its narrow sense of dogma and rituals. The Buddha gave simple and scientific ways for peace, happiness, and to attain *nirvāṇa*. All this is possible through *bhāvanā*.[2] So, Buddhist *bhāvanā* is mental culture or mental development in the full sense of the term. It aims at cleansing the mind of impurities and disturbances such as lustful desires, hatred, ill-will, indolence, worries, and restlessness. It aims at cultivating qualities like concentration, awareness, intelligence, will, and tranquillity. All this ultimately leads one to the attainment of the highest wisdom which would help us know the nature of things as they are.

Buddhism is a plan of living in such a way as to derive the most out of life. The Buddha did not preach to win converts but to enlighten listeners. Buddhism is always 'a question of knowing and seeing, and not of believing'.

The Buddha stressed that the right to question should never be given up. He said that one must never take anyone's word as the ultimate truth. For, what is true today may not be true tomorrow. Therefore, he exhorted his disciples to 'culture and the development of a questioning mind'. The Buddha gave the world the Four Noble Truths: "suffering, origin of suffering, cessation of suffering, and way to cessation". These, coupled with his Eight-Fold Path, are the key to success and satiation. In this life, our means of livelihood should be honest and not at the cost

---

2. *Bhāvanā*, used repeatedly in Buddhist scriptures, is a Pāli word, and it means culture or mental development.

of others. In the pursuit of success, one should not cause any harm to others. Our behaviour and speech should not be offensive. Compassion, understanding, good intentions, right action, right livelihood, and right effort are the key words around which Buddhism revolves.

2

Development of Buddhist Tantra

In outward appearance, the Buddhist Tantra are similar to the Hindu Tantra. But there is no similarity between the two either in subject or in philosophical doctrines embodied in them. The aim and objects of the Buddhist religion are widely different from those of the Hindu religion. It is difficult to determine when and under what circumstances the word *tantra* was used, nor it is possible to trace the person who first introduced them. It will be evident that when the mystical practices become popular with one section of society, the other section incorporates in its religion in a modified form to suit its own requirements and tenets. So, that Tantrism existed from very early times and was transmitted in the most secret manner possible from time to time. So, it can be seen that Tantrism was handed down from the most secret manner possible before its followers could swell in number so as to openly declare themselves and preach their doctrine.

Unfortunately, we do not possess any connected account except a few works on the *Dhāraṇīs*. Buddhist Tantra belong to Mahāyāna and not to Hīnayāna. The Buddhist Tantra were a development of the Yogācāra school which evolved out of *śūnyavāda* of Mādhyamikas. The Buddhist Tantra were an outcome of Mahāyāna, and is known as Vajrayāna.

The Buddha found enlightenment, and out of his infinite compassion taught the way of salvation which he had discovered. The world is a place of suffering, if for no other reason then for the reason that its joys are transient and all lives end in decay and death. All creatures are suffering in an endless cycle. The Buddha said that physical and mental constituents kept going by desire. It is desire alone which leads to rebirth. Gnosis is to realise this and act accordingly. So, people should eliminate desire and attain salvation. All living beings are equally entitled to respect and love. Salvation consists in a state of blissful calm so long as this life lasts, and no rebirth when it comes to an end.

Tāntric practices in Buddhism are old. These practices were found in abundance as references, as early Buddhist literature indicates. The attitude of Buddhism seems to have been against such practices, but at the same time, there were some mystic practices, thought to be harmless, which were tolerated. Buddha is said to have expressed his great disapprobation of Tantra or Tāntric practices. He did not permit the consumption of fish, meat, wine, and association with the opposite sex in the church among other things. The result was that during the lifetime of Buddha, many monks revolted against his injunctions; there were many others who did not openly revolt against the Buddha's injunctions, but nevertheless, violated them in secret. The result was that, there arose secret conclaves of Buddhists, who, though professing to be monks, secretly practised what was disapproved by the Buddha and His followers, and disallowed in practice. After the death of Buddha, the spirit of revolution, which served as a very kernel of all Buddhistic thought and religion, was distorted as a result of slow but continued friction with current Hindu thoughts and practices. As a result, there seems to have developed a spirit of compromise. This spirit of compromise, combined with the Mahāyānic spirit of catholicity in throwing the portals of Buddhism wide open to people of various tastes, was responsible for the absorption of many of important Hindu practices into Buddhism itself. This indicates the process by which Tāntricism made its way into Buddhism. The mission of Buddha to wean the Indian mind from the blind faith in worship and rituals passed into oblivion. The tradition of worship of the divinities, mystical utterances, and *yogic* practices led to the growth of esotericism, which in course of time became Tāntricism.

It is easy to argue that where Buddhism is concerned, Tantrism was a natural growth owing to circumstances favourable to this kind of development. Hinduism, too, had a primitive kind of magic in the form of rituals and ceremonies, but these were not practised in secret. The secret Buddhist conclaves that grew on the ruins of monastic order, developed, in course of time, into big organisations known as Guhyasamāja that held their teachings and practices in secret (*guhya*). Thus, the *Guhyasamāja-tantra* was composed in the *saṁgīti* form (collection of verses). It explained why the teachings of school were kept secret for so long, and how even a devout Buddhist could practise all that was enjoined as Tantra, together with details of theories and practices about rituals. It is argued that when Buddha came to the world as Dipaṁkara and Kāśyapa, he did not preach these secret doctrines because in those days people were not found fit to receive such instructions. But, they have made the secret doctrines public as the people were prepared to receive such initiations. Its most important declaration was that the emancipation does not depend on bodily sufferings and abstinence from the worldly enjoyments; that perfection cannot be obtained through processes which are difficult and painful, but only through the satisfaction of all desires. Its teaching in this respect is direct and unequivocal. In early days, the rules and regulations prescribed for followers of Hīnayāna and Mahāyāna were unduly severe, as they thought about much hardships and bodily sufferings. The attainment of Buddhahood was an arduous task that took a long time or even many births. In contrast, Guhyasamāja introduced a process by which Buddhahood could be attained within the shortest time possible, and even in a single birth by indulging in all sorts of enjoyment. Another element introduced in Buddhism was that of Śakti (women considered as manifestations of divine energy) for obtaining emancipation through *yoga* and *samādhi*. The Buddha was transformed in the form of 'five *dhyānī* Buddhas' and each of them was associated with Śakti. Buddhahood was seen as impossible by any means if one did not recognise *prajñā* (*vidyā*) or *śakti*. The worldly phenomena was actually non-dual in essence, though, it appeared to be dual.

It is said that Tantric elements in Buddhism were introduced by Lord Buddha himself. Buddha did not fail to notice the importance of incorporating magical practices in his religion. Belief in *mantra* or in the mysterious power of sound is a social heritage with the Indian people from the ancient past. Such a belief in various forms is to be occasionally found in early Buddhism. Worship of *stūpa*, reverence for the mystic *bodhimaṇḍala*, or circle round the famous tree beneath which Buddha attained his *bodhi* (perfect knowledge) were also popular features of early Buddhism. The posture and gesture of Buddha were also held mystically significant. These are elements in early Buddhism which no doubt paved the way for the vigorous propagation of the *mantra*, *mudrā* and *maṇḍala* elements in Tāntric Buddhism. Effacement of self was the keynote of all Indian religions, and it was one of the basic teachings of Buddha. It was taken by the Hīnayānists in a very practical manner in their monastic system of life, the object of which was to make the inmates rise above all cares and anxieties for the well-being of their own selves. It was inculcated through meditational exercises which helped their minds to realise that one's body was a store-house of impurities. The exercises made the Hīnayānists oblivious of their own selves and taught themselves abnegation. The Hīnayānists conceived of Buddha at first as an omniscient human being; then, in course of time, attributed to him superhuman even superdivine powers and qualities, and regarded him as superior to all beings. To the Mahāyānist, this procedure for effacement of self appeared totally wrong and wholly inadequate. They approach the problem from a totally different angle of vision. According to them, the effacement of self could only be effected by dedicating one's own life in his several existences to the service of others. A Mahāyānist must take the vow that he could not seek his own happiness, heavenly life, even *nirvāṇa*, unless and until he had been able to do his bit to make all other beings happy, attain heavenly life, and ultimately realise *nirvāṇa*. This altruistic attitude was the keynote of the Mahāyānist system which regarded Buddha as eternal without origin and decay, the truth, the end of existence (*bhūtakoṭi*), and as such beyond any description whatsoever. Thereby, the Master turned into Lord.

Though, both accepted the common code of monastic rules yet there was wide divergence regarding the doctrines and ideals of the two schools. The Hīnayānists were more realistic, while Mahāyānists were pure negativists or idealists. The difference hinged on the interpretation of *śūnyatā* (*anātmatā*), a term, frequently used by Buddha without a clear definition. By this term, the Hīnayānists understood the non-existence of any real substance as man or individuality (*pudgala-śūnyatā*). While the Mahāyānists took it to be the non-existence of individuality (*pudgala* or *ātman*) as also of the objective world (*dharma*). According to Mahāyāna, the truth is *śūnyatā* (which is attributeless), negation of being and non-being or *tathatā* (the state of sameness, i.e., of noumenon) or *dharma-dhātu* (totality of phenomenal manifestations, the universe or universal principle) which is identified with *nirvāṇa* of Buddha.

The aim of the Hīnayānists was to attain *arthat-hood* through *nirvāṇa*, to be liberated from cycle of birth and death. An *arhat* is an ideal person who is free from all worldy things. The conception of *arthat-hood* is negated in Mahāyāna, and is substituted by that of *bodhisattva*-hood. And final extinction through *nirvāṇa* is not the ultimate goal of the Mahāyānists, their aim is to become a *bodhisattva*. The whole of Mahāyāna literature breaths this spirit of universal compassion with the intention of rendering help to the affiliated in getting rid of their applications. The aim of Mahāyāna is mass-salvation, and that is why it claims itself to be the great (*mahā*) vehicle. And this universal compassion was one of the most important factors that popularised Buddhism that had spread in lands far and wide, and gave the religion a deep humanitarianation and easily attract the sympathy and attention of people of different tests and temperaments. This Mahāyānic spirit exerted a great influence in shaping the general religious attitude of Tāntric Buddhism.

Buddha took it for granted that all that is contained in the world is impermanent, and therefore, full of misery. He promulgated the noble

Eight-Fold Path which may give freedom from the miseries of birth and death. *Nirvāṇa* was the goal of human life. *Nirvāṇa* is like the extinguishing of a lamp. As the lamp is extinguished when there is no more oil, so man gets *nirvāṇa* when he has no more suffering (*kleśa*). This explanation of *nirvāṇa* is as given in Hīnayāna. Nāgārjuna, the founder of the Mādhyamika system of philosophy explained the condition of mind in *nirvāṇa* as *śūnya* and described it as a condition about which neither existence nor non-existence nor a combination of the two nor a negation of the two can be predicated.[1] The followers of the Yogācāra school were not satisfied with this explanation of *śūnya* which as described by Mādhyamika is an indescribable condition. They wanted to have a positive element is *śūnya*; and that positive element is *vijñāna* of which the individual is composed. The chain of development of the idea of *nirvāṇa* came to a termination in the Tāntric age when the element of *mahāsukha* entered into the conception of *nirvāṇa*. People thought the life of a saint was of foregoing the pleasures of life. After the goal was attained there remained either a questionable existence as formulated in *śūnyavāda* or simple *vijñāna* as formulated in the Yogācāra.[2] The *mahāsukhavādins* satisfied all by holding out a promise that even when *nirvāṇa* is attained there remains something and that something is *vijñāna*, continually to remain in eternal bliss and happiness. They said *śūnya* is *nirātmā*, and *bodhicitta* in the embrace of *nirātmā* remains in eternal bliss and happiness.[3] Though, this new

1. In brief, the above is the Mahāyānic idealistic standpoint with which popular cults and rituals have been curiously blended. A devotional religion with the Buddha as the highest god who is eternal, without any origin and decay, and ultimate reality which is beyond any sort of description, was grafted into the frame of the *śūnya* doctrine of Mahāyāna.
2. The Yogācāra theory of *vijñāna* or consciousness being akin to Tāntric belief of superiority of spirit to the matter, paved the way for *sādhanā* and *siddhi*; by such *siddhi* one attains supernatural power. Such practices are traced to the Guhyasamāja, assigned to Asaṅga (third century AD).
3. When the *bodhicitta* (will to enlightenment) mingles with *śūnya* or the infinite spirit, in the highest state of meditation, the mind is filled with innumerable visions and scenes; then the *sādhaka* visualises the germ-syllables, which gradually assume the shape of deities, first indistinct then changing into perfect →

introduction appealed to the advanced Buddhists, it weakened to a great extent the religion morally, and the degeneration of Buddhism started from this point and developed into the Tāntric Buddhism.[4]

The theory of *karuṇā* required that the *bodhisattva* should sacrifice everything, his happiness and even his own merits and salvation, for the suffering humanity. He must work hard through a continuous chain of births and deaths for the emancipation of his fellow beings. This ideal, which is entirely absent in Hīnayāna, was probably introduced in the first century AD. This idea of *karuṇā* is unique in the history of Buddhism, and Buddhist religion can very well be proud of this one single conception. But this ideal was too much for them. They could neither assimilate it, nor practise it, nor realise its importance. The result was that the vow to emancipate the whole world was turned into a mere convention; and one will be surprised to find that Vajrayānists took shelter under its cover and found in it an excuse for committing acts of great immorality. In Vajrayāna, easy methods leading to happiness in this world, were held out to the people, and easy paths leading to salvation were shown. The religious regulations (disciplinary) slackened down one after another, and ultimately, Vajrayānists gained much power. The followers of the Vajrayāna, however, justify their action under the shelter of *karuṇā* theory and say that there is nothing that cannot be done by one who has sacrificed everything for the emancipation of the world.

According to the Mahāyāna conception, *śūnyatā* or perfect wisdom, and *karuṇā*, or universal compassion, generate in one's mind the

---

→ glorious and living form, the embodiment of *śūnya*. The *Advaya-vajra-saṁgraha* says, "From the right perception of *śūnya* proceed the germ-syllables, from the germ-syllables proceeds the conception of image, and from the image its external representation. The whole process is, therefore, of dependent origination (*pratītyasamutpāda*). Thus, the deities have no, as such, external form but represent the purely mental conception." (*Advaya-vajra-saṁgraha*, pp. 50-1)

4. The Mahāyāna Buddhism is entirely different from what Buddha originally taught, but the Buddhism of the Tāntric period is much more different from the Mahāyāna Buddhism. If the Buddhism taught by the Buddha and the Buddhism of the Tāntric period (Vajrayāna) are placed side by side, one will find not even remote connection between the two.

bodhicitta, a state in which one is free from all worldliness. The *bodhicitta* next proceeds on an upward march, through ten different stages (*bhūmis*), and when the last stage is reached, one becomes a perfect *bodhisattva*. Tāntric Buddhism interprets the whole thing in a different way. Here *śunyatā* is identified with *prajñā*, the female principle, and *karuṇā* with *upāya*, the male, and it is held that the inner union of the two produces supreme bliss. Since, the human body is the abode of Buddha, and also the epitome of the universe, liberation must come through the action of the body alone (*kāya-sādhanā*), and this gross sex pleasure can even lead one to the realisation of the ultimate reality. With the identification of *prajñā* and *upāya* with the female and male principle respectively, the idea of Śakti and Śiva was established in the Buddhist Tantra. From a metaphysical point of view, *prajñā* is the passive spectator, while *upāya* or *karuṇā* are active agents that stir up waves of mentation in *prajñā*. This idea seems to be closely akin to the popular Sāṁkhya view, and thus metaphysical significance of *prajñā* and *upāya* has a close bearing on the coneption of Śakti and Śiva. The only difference is that in Śāktism, the male spirit (Śiva or *puruṣa*) is the passive spectator whose existence is necessary to stir up energy in *prakṛti* (Śakti or female pirinciple), and it is *prakṛti* (Śakti) that is the only active force.

Mahāyāna Buddhism was subdivided into two distinct schools the Mantrayāna and Pāramitāyāna. The former seems to be the introductory stage from which other offshoots like Vajrayāna, Kālacakrayāna and Sahajayāna, etc., arose in later times. Vajrayāna is probably due to its relation with the term *vajra* in place of *śunyatā*, i.e., the void nature of the self and all entities. According to this school, the ultimate reality is *vajrasattva* who is the Primal elightened one, Ādi-Buddha, possessed of five kinds of knowledge as attributes that give rise to five *dhyānī* Buddhas. About the tenth century AD, the Kālacakrayāna school developed within the fold of Vajrayāna, the Supreme Deity of which is Śrī-Kālacakra. *Kāla* represents *prajñā* and *cakra*, *upāya*, and thus, *kālacakra* implies the absolute union of female and male principles. Sahajayāna, on the other hand, was a revolutionary form which denied all conventionalism, ceremonialism, and muttering of *mantra* of

Vajrayāna. The *sahajīya* Buddhists adopted human nature itself as the best appliance for realising the truth, and hence, they called their path the easiest and the most natural (*sahaja*). The real origin of the cult lies more outside Buddhism than inside it. The Buddhist *sahaja* cult, notwithstanding the Buddhist tone and colour which it assumes; is essentially an esoteric *yogic* cult. Side by side, with the commonly known theological speculations and religious practices, there has been flowing in India an important religious undercurrent of esoteric *yogic* practices from a pretty old time. These esoteric practices, when associatd with the theological speculation of Śaivas and the Śāktas, have given rise to the Śaiva and Śākta Tāntricism; when associated with Buddhist speculations these esoteric practices have given rise to the composite religious system of Buddhist Tāntricism, and, again, when associated with the speculations of Bengal Vaiṣṇavism, the same esoteric practices have been responsible for the growth of the esoteric Vaiṣṇavite cult, known of the Vaiṣṇava Sahajīyas that never prescribes any unnatural strain on human nature. Great importance is laid on human body which is believed to be abode of truth and also the medium of realising the truth. The bliss is produced through the union of the male and the female symbolising *prajñā* and *upāya*, i.e., the *bodhicitta* is conceived as *sahaja* or the innate nature of self and the world around. *Prajñā* or the goddess manifests herself in every woman, and every man is the embodiment of *upāya*, the male principle, and their union alone can produce supreme bliss. In the *caryā* songs, we find mention of this female principle, and there is also frequent mention of the union of the aspirant with this personified female deity.

The religion lost itself in the maze of mysticism, and was engulfed by a host of *mudrā*s, *maṇḍala*s, *kriyā*s, and *charyā*s. The teaching of one of the noblest minds was thus deformed into a system of magical spells, exorcisms, spirit-beliefs, and worship of demons and divinities. This new-phased religion, in which original ethical philosophical principles were superimposed in such a way by an esoteric yogic system, combined with endless rituals and forms of worship, that it could hardly be called Buddhism any longer.

3

Religious Outlook

THE development of Tantrism effected a radical change in the outlook and character of Indian religion, which aimed at the salvation of all by the spirit of universal love for all mankind. It yielded to gross superstitions and immoral practices so far as the general masses were concerned. Esoteric practices as the easiest means for attaining salvation, with the conception of ultimate reality as a duality of male and female energy, paved the way for erotic and sensual practices and undermined the sense of moral values. Actually, the fundamental principles of Tantra were conceived by great minds with the best intentions, but the way advised for salvation was very dangerous to the ordinary people, most of them (devotee) fell victims to temptation and perished on the way before they could reach the land of bliss; the most regrettable feature was degradation in ideas of morality brought by Tāntric religion. This evil corroded the whole society. Even then, the esoteric character of Tāntric religion limited its field; and those forms of religious practices were made exceptional and normal. We have to admit that the poorer and higher forms of religious ideas and practices continued to flourish among higher classes in India. Tantra primarily intended to expound practical methods for the realisation of the ultimate truth.

The religious history of this period is the triumphant revival of Brāhmaṇical religion that extended its dominant position over the whole of India. The growth of temples constitutes an important feature in the development of religion in India. Rich endowments made those temples as important centres of education, missionary activity, and spiritual inspiration. The *maṭhas* and *vihāras* which grew up in large numbers, not only supplemented these activities, but also took humanitarian stands like feeding the poor and tending the sick. The period under review witnessed not only the decadence of Buddhism but also the appearance of a new phase of the religion in which original, ethical, and philosophical principles were superimposed in such a way by an esoteric yogic system, combined with endless rituals and form of worship, that it could hardly be called Buddhism any longer. The mission of Buddha to wean the Indian mind from blind faith in worship and rituals passed into oblivion. Buddha's rational and ethical teachings, free from worship and rituals, gradually gave way in the early centuries of the Christian era to a popular form of religion with a new ethical devotional outlook, while his philosophical teachings received a new interpretation and ended the glorious days of Buddhist logic and philosophy. The promulgators of the new system sought their justification from the ancient words of Buddha and the philosophical teachings of Asaṅga and Nāgārjuna. However, it must be admitted that this new type of *sādhanā* (yogic practices) did confer on the adepts some superhuman powers and also led many to the realisation of high spiritual states; this new phase of Buddhism envisaged something very deep and subtle to be realised only by those who were initiated into the secrets by their spiritual teachers. It must be admitted that the human mind can be worked up into any type of perversity, that in the name of religion and philosophy, necessity and circumstances debased human mind to the lowest conceivable vulgarity.

According to Mahāyāna, every human being is a potential Buddha and within himself he has all the possibilities of becoming a Samyak-Sambuddha (the perfect enlightened one). The liberation of all people being the sacred pledge of Mahāyāna, it is the religion for all with the spirit of benevolence and humanity. The doctrine of universal compassion (*karuṇā*) was adopted and utilised by Tāntric Buddhists. They professed with the purpose of saving the world from miseries; and all their mystic rites and practices did bear the impress of *karuṇā* on them. It may be said that this Mahāyāna doctrine of *karuṇā* was directly or indirectly responsible for introducing Tāntricism in Buddhism. *Karuṇā* (universal compassion) is called *upāya*, because it is a medium for the attainment of *bodhicitta* for the realisation of the highest goal. *Śūnyatā* is *prajñā*, because it represents perfect wisdom (knowledge of the void-nature of the self and the *dharma*). *Prajñā* or *śūnyatā* (perfect knowledge) represents a static or negative state of mind which separates the individual from the world of suffering beings; it makes one to observe the world of existence from a point of view where there is neither suffering nor happiness and no opportunity left for displaying the spirit of benevolence; it makes a man altogether static. On the other hand, *upāya* or *karuṇā*, operates in one's mind like a dynamic force, draws one's attention to the world of suffering, and as the symbol of universal compassion removes the miseries of the suffering world. *Prajñā* or *śūnyatā*, standing for perfect wisdom, is regarded as absolutely passive and negative aspect of the reality. While *karuṇā* or *upāya*, with its active inspiration and because of its dynamic nature, is conceived as the active and positive aspect of the same. The nature of *prajñā* is non-existence, and that of *upāya*, existence; *prajñā* is essencelessness, while *upāya* is of positive nature; so the whole truth is the unity of both these positive and negative aspects. So, the *bodhicitta*, is the unified state of *śūnyatā* and *karuṇā*.[1]

1. The conception of *śūnyatā* and *karuṇā* of Mahāyāna Buddhism later developed into those of *prajñā* and *upāya* of Tāntric Buddhism symbolising the female and male principles respectively. *Prajñā* is viewed as a goddess (Bhagavatī). The term is also used to denote *mudrā* technically a woman to be adopted for the purpose of ritual. Again in some places *prajñā* is the word for the female organ which is the seat of all pleasures (*mahāsukha*). *Upāya* and *prajñā* are also called the *vajra* (thunder) and the *padma* (lotus) respectively, the former symbolising the male organ (*maṇi, liṅga*) and the latter the female (*yoni*).

   The Tāntric Buddhists developed a theology of their own, which is different from the philosophy and religion of canonical Buddhism. According to these esoteric Buddhists, *bodhicitta* is the highest truth, it is the absolute. It is the

→

According to the Mahāyāna conception, *śūnyatā* or perfect wisdom and *karuṇā*, or universal compassion, generate in one's mind the *bodhicitta*, a state in which one is free from all worldliness. The *bodhicitta* next proceeds on an upward march, through ten different stages (*bhūmis*), and when the last stage is reached one becomes a perfect *bodhisattva*. Tāntric Buddhism interprets the whole thing in a different way. Here *śūnyatā* is identified with *prajñā*, the female principle, and *karuṇā* with *upāya*, the male, and it is held that the inner union of the two produces supreme bliss. Since the human body is the abode of Buddha, and also the epitome of the universe, liberation must come through the action of the body alone (*kāya-sādhanā*), and thus, gross sex pleasure can even lead one to the realisation of the ultimate reality. With the identification of *prajñā* and *upāya* with the female and male principles respectively, the idea of Śakti and Śiva was established in the Buddhist Tantra.[2] This

---

→ *sahaja*, the innate nature of the self and the world. This *bodhicitta* is explained as a unified state of *śūnyatā* (void) and *karuṇā* (universal compassion). *Karuṇā* is a strong emotion of compassion, it is the dynamic principle that leads one to an active life for the liberation not only of one's self but also of others; it is therefore, the active principle and is called *upāya* (the means). *Prajñā,* as pure consciousness (*vijñapti-mātratā*) or pure wisdom, represents the domain of *nivṛtti*, while *upāya*, as the active principle, represents the domain of *pravṛtti*. If we examine the practices of Tāntric Buddhism, we shall find that the final aim in all such cases was the attainment of an infinitely blissful state of *samādhi*, through the absorbing emotion of love or sex-pleasure. In a unique flow of intensely blissful realisation, uninterrupted by the notions of subjectivity and objectivity, there is an infinite oneness in the mind, which is said to be the state of unity of emotion (*samarasa*); when all the subjective and objective disturbances of the mind are absolutely lost in a supreme realisation of bliss, we attain our trueself, which is *samādhi* (*sahaja*) or *samarasa*.

2. According to Hindu Tantra, the Absolute Reality (which is neutral by nature) has two aspects within it, *nivṛtti* and *pravṛtti* which may be rendered as static and dynamic, or as negative and positive. In Tantras, these are generally conceived of as Śiva and Śakti. Śiva is pure consciousness, qualityless, and, as such, the static or the negative principle, while Śakti is cosmic energy, the world force, and, as such, the dynamic or the positive aspect of reality. But, neither Śiva by himself nor Śakti by herself is the ultimate truth; they are not even separated, the highest truth is the state of neutrality produced through the union of Śiva and Śakti, which under one condition, produces the highest state of neutrality in infinite bliss, and produces, under different conditions, the world →

ultimate state of non-duality, or the destruction of all principles of dualism, is called by the Tāntric Buddhism, the state of *yuganaddha*, *advaya*, *samarasa*, etc. Once reaching the stage of *yuganaddha*,[3] one attains perfect enlightenment and eternal tranquillity and crosses the sea of birth and death. This is in fact perfect enlightenment of *buddhattva*, and this is the way in which innumerable Buddhas attained perfection. The Tāntric Buddhists' conception is that the male and female represent in this world *upāya* and *prajñā*, the union of which is the highest reality. As such, to obtain the highest spiritual experience, men and women must first of all realise themselves as manifestations of *upāya* and *prajñā*, and be united together in body, mind, and spirit. The supreme bliss that emerges from that union is the highest religious gain. All esoteric *sādhanā* must, therefore, be performed by the male and female together, and this is the easy process of realising the right truth. The Lord Buddha, was the incarnation of *upāya*, and his wife (Gopā), Prajñā, and the Buddha attained supreme bliss (*mahāsukha*) of the nature of *nirvāṇa* in union with Prajñā (Gopā). In the Buddhist Tantra, *prajñā* (the female aspect of absolute) is viewed as Bhagavatī (goddess); it is also a term often used to imply the *mudrā*; she is also called *vajra-kanyā*. *Prajñā* and *upāya*, as the symbol of the female and male, are also called, respectively, the *padma* (lotus) and the *vajra* (thunder), the former symbolising the female and the latter the male organ.

→ manifestation, or the phenomenon of process as a whole. When Śakti associated with all her principles of illusion and defilement dominates, the union of Śiva and Śakti, which takes place in the realm of *pravṛtti*, becomes responsible for the causation of the visible world, but when Śakti rises to Śiva in a process of introversion, their union results in a state of neutrality in infinite bliss and tranquillity. So, the union that binds may also liberate. This *tattva* of Śiva-Śakti lies within the body of man. Man represents Śiva and woman represents Śakti, the perfect bliss that results from a strict discipline and yogic control of their union leads one to perfect tranquillity which is the state of the Absolute.

3. *Yuganaddha* is also described as the non-dual state and is identified with the *bodhicitta*, and it is defined as a state of absolute non-duality marked by the absence of notions like worldly process and cessation of that process (*nivṛtti*), adherence (*saṁkleśa*) and distinction (*vyavadhāna*), and perceivable and perceiver (*grāhya* and *grāhaka*). H.V. Gunther, *Yuganaddha*, T.N. Mishra, *Impact of Tantra of Religion and Art*, p. 90.

The esoteric *sādhanā* involving the physical and psychological union of the *prajñā* and *upāya* leads to the inner union of the two, and through this yogic union is produced supreme bliss (*mahāsukha*),[4] which, according to the Buddhist Tantra, is the very nature of the absolute. One realises the absolute only when one realises one's ownself as perfect bliss. The ultimate end is, therefore, to attain this state of perfect bliss. In our ordinary life, we do feel like experiences, intense pleasure in our sex-experiences, but between the sex-pleasure and perfect bliss, which constitutes the ultimate nature of our self, there is an abyss of difference. The experiences of sex-pleasure, extremely transitory and of defiled character as they are, only fasten us to a lower plane of life. But the sexo-yogic *sādhanā* of Tāntrics is a *sādhanā* which is calculated to be capable of transmitting.

> even gross sex-pleasure into the realisation of infinite bliss in which all the activities of the mind are absolutely lost, and in which the self and world around are lost in an all-pervading oneness.

This is what is reckoned as *nirvāṇa* by the Tāntric Buddhist.

With the identification of *mahāsukha* with *nirvāṇa* and the principles of *prajñā* and *upāya* with the female and male organs, the Mahāyāna concept of *bodhicitta* was destined to undergo a thorough change in Tāntric Buddhism. The *bodhicitta* is no more the state of mind in which there reigns only strong determination to attain perfect wisdom (*bodhi*), but it signifies the production of an extremely blissful state of mind through the yogic union of the two (male and female). This is further elaborated by the identification of different philosophical concepts with various parts of the nervous system of the human body and the conception of the attainment of the final bliss as a physical process.

According to esoteric Buddhists, the body is the abode of truth and

---

4. The character of *mahāsukha* is described in *Jñānasiddhi*, ch. VII; see two Vajrayāna works, *G.O.S.*, No. XLIV, p. 57; this new idea was known as the Mahāsukhavāda, and the form of Buddhism which was based on this Mahāsukhavāda was known as Vajrayāna, or the adamant vehicle.

at the same time, the best medium for realising the truth. With this belief, it located four plexuses (lotuses) in different parts of the body along the spinal column.[5] The first is *nirmāṇa-cakra* situated in the naval region, representing the *nirmāṇa-kāya* or the principal of material transformations or created body, also known as *rūpa-kāya*; this body is generally for guidance of common worldly men and beings. He assumes an earthly form which is subject to all human frailties. According to Mahāyānists, Gautama Buddha, is the *nirmāṇa-kāya* of the real Buddha. The second is the *dharma-cakra* situated in the cardiac region, representing the *dharma-kāya*, or the principle of non-dual cosmic existence, the universal principle, which has no form, is infinite and external without appearance or disappearance. The third is the *saṁbhoga-cakra* situated near the neck, representing the *saṁbhoga-kāya* or the principle of the body of bliss. Buddha assumed a refulgent

5. The whole Tāntric *sādhanā* was based on the cardinal belief that the truth is to be realised through the body of man. The belief of *tāntrikas* is that the ultimate truth is not an abstract principle transcending the universe, but is immanent in it, and that the human body is not merely a thing in the universe, but is an epitome of the universe — a microcosm in relation to the macrocosm. There is, therefore, nothing in the universe which is not there in the body of man. There is perfect parallelism between physical process of the universe and the biological processes in the body of man. With this idea, the tantra tries to locate the world within the human body. The implication seems to be that the human body, with its physical structure and biological processes, represents the manifestation of the same energy which is at play in the structure and process of the cosmos. The human form is, therefore, the abode of truth of which the universe is a manifestation in infinite space and eternal time. Instead of being lost in the mystery of the incomprehensible universe, the *sādhaka* should concentrate his attention on himself and realise the truth within, with the clear conviction that the truth that is realised within is the truth that pervades the universe without.

   Haṭha-yoga is a remarkable factor in Tāntric practices, and the *haṭha-yogic* practices are those through which the body is transformed into the best medium or instrument for realising the truth. According to Tāntric *yogins*, different plexuses, nerves, and nerve-centres represent different *tattvas*; but *tattvas* represented by them lie latent until they are made potent through proper yogic culture and control. This subtle analysis of the physical (including the biological) system of man and formulation of process, through which this physical system may be transformed into a perfect instrument for reflecting the truth, constitute the best contribution of the tantra.

richly adorned form with all the signs of great men, for the satisfaction of his devotees. This body is called *sambhoga-kāya* because it is known as the special acquisition of Buddha on account of merits accumulated in several lives. Above all these, and transcending all these, is the plexus (lotus) in the head, which is the seat of absolute truth. An additional nervous-cycle is *uṣṇīśa kamala* in the central region which is the symbol of the Buddha, *vajra-kāya* or *sahaja-kāya* and which corresponds to the Śākta concepts of *sahasrāra*. The cosmic energy (conceived as a feminine principle) remains as a fire-force in the *nirmāṇa-cakra*,[6] and here associated with all gross principles of difilement, she acts the principle of phenomenalism. She must be roused and dissociated from all principles of difilement and given an upward motion, so as to reach the *uṣṇīśa kamala*, which is the region of perfect purity.[7] Again the important nerve on the left side of the body, called moon or the river Gaṅgā, represents *prajñā*, the woman, and the nerve on the right side, called Sun or the river Yamunā, represents *upāya*, the Lord (ovum being the symbol for the goddess and seed for the Lord). The left and the right should be controlled and commingled in such a way that all the functions (including the flow of the vital currents *prāṇa* and *apāna* in the two nerves) may be completely unified in the middle path, called *avadhūti* (*avadhūti* has been explained in Buddhist texts as that which, through its effulgent nature, destroys all sin), such a perfect unification, resulting, ultimately, in the realisation of infinite bliss (*mahāsukha*), which is the quintessence

6. S.B. Dasgupta, *Obscure Religious Cults*, pp. 211-55.

7. In Buddhist Tantra the semen called *bodhicitta* (the name of *bodhicitta* given to semen) implies the degeneration of the spiritual message of the Master, who was in favour of celibacy. It was also believed in the later stage of Buddhism that 'Buddhahood lies in the female generative organ'. The fall of the semen is considered a great sin. The semen must not be emitted, for otherwise the *yogin* falls under the Law of Time and Death. For checking the flow of semen, the *sādhaka* practices coitus reservations by taking recource to *Haṭha-yoga* or the psychophysical technique. The semen instead of flowing downward is led by *yoga* to the highest centre of the body or the *uṣṇīsa-kamala* of Buddhist Tantra. Nagendra Nath Upadhyay, *Tantric Bauddha Sādhanā aur Sāhitya*, pp. 315; *Haṭhayogapradipikā*, by Pancham Singh, III, 83-88; T.N. Mishra, *Impact of Tantra on Religion and Art*, pp. 94, 96.

of the *bodhicitta*. Prajñā (the goddess) manifests herself in every woman, and every man is the embodiment of Upāya, the Lord.

In the actual *sādhanā*, the man and the woman must first of all transcend their corporal existence and realise their true self as *upāya* and *prajñā* respectively. With such a realisation they should unite and control the sex act in such a way that the downward motion of seed may be arrested and an upward motion given to it till it reaches the highest plexus and remains there motionless.[8] This motionless state of the seed in the highest plexus conduces to infinite bliss and tranquillity, and realisation of the highest bliss is realisation of the highest truth, for bliss is the ultimate nature of truth. *Prajñopāya* (*prjñā* and *upāya*) is, therefore, equivalent to *mahāsukha* (supreme bliss) and entirely auspicious (*sāmantabhadra*). The state of perfection is neither duality nor non-duality. Wisdom conceived as the female is to be combined in one's ownself for the purpose of liberation which is perfect enlightenment through the practical experience of the female principle. *Prajñā* or wisdom is linked with a state of intense emotion called *sukha* (bliss) or *mahāsukha* (great bliss) which is conducive to complete enlightenment. *Prajñā* is often identified in flesh and blood with a woman, and the concept of *mahāsukha* is sought to be explained in terms of sexual symbolism, which is in general agreement with the common Tāntric

---

8. The highest joy that ensues from the coital act is only momentary or ephemeral with the discharge of semen; its normal downward flow when checked and reversed by the *yogī* towards the seat of consciousness in the lotus the 'return of semen' — marks the emanation of the Supreme Bliss that is permanent, and the cause of immortality. Thus, it is *śukram* or 'semen virile' that is sometimes described as the Supreme Bliss. In the *Hevajra-tantra*, the Lord Buddha himself says, I am existence, I am not existence. I am the Enlightened one for I am enlightened about what things are. My nature is that of *sahaja* bliss and I come at the end of joy of cessation (*virāmānanda*). I am the Lord with thirty-two marks, the Lord with eighty characteristics. I dwell in the *sukhāvatī* of the *bhaga* (vagina) of woman, and my form is *śukram* (semen) — without that (i.e., *śukram*) there is no bliss, and without bliss this would not be. Since one can never be effective without the other, bliss ensues only in union with the female divinity. *Hevajra-tantra*, ed. and tr. D.L. Snellgrove, Vol. I and II pp. 48-50; T.N. Mishra, *Impact of Tantra on Religion and Art*, pp. 85, 90.

tradition. The highest state of the union of the two is that of supreme love and it is the real *sahaja mahāsukha*.

The union of *prajñā* and *upāya* through the principle of *yuganaddha* for the purpose of the realisation of the non-dual state, symbolised by the physical union of the adept and his female partner, brings in succession *rāga* and *mahā-rāga* (emotion and intense emotion, evidently transcendental, resulting from a genuine feeling of compassion); *samarasa* (oneness of a motion) is in which there is no cognition of *prajñā* and *upāya*, and finally, the *mahāsukha* or great bliss which is of the nature of the absolute unity of *prajñā* and *upāya*, the non-dual quintessence of all the entities without which perfect wisdom is never possible.

The final aim in all such cases was the attainment of an infinitely blissful state of arrest (*samādhi*) either purely through a psycho-physiological process of *yoga* or through the absorbing emotion of love, strictly disciplined and intensified through the practice of *yoga*. Intense human love, or sexual pleasure, thus transformed beyond recognition, has the capacity to produce a supreme state of arrest. In a unique flow of intensely blissful realisation, uninterrupted by the notions of subjectivity and objectivity, there dawns an infinite oneness in the mind, which is said to be the state of unity of emotion (*samarasa*). All the subjective and objective disturbances of the mind are absolutely lost in a supreme realisation of bliss and in that state, we attain our true self, which is *sahaja*. To judge this state of *samarasa* or *sahaja* as a pure state of *samādhi*, a *sādhaka* practises *yoga* in the plane of mind (*citta-bhūmi*).

To understand the rise of Vajrayāna, it is necessary to go back to the original teachings of the Buddha. The Lord Buddha prescribed two *yāna*s in the beginning, namely, the Śrāvakayāna and the Pratyeka-Buddhayāna. The Śrāvakas were to hear from a Buddha, they could not attain *nirvāṇa* themselves, but they had to wait till the advent of another Buddha for their emancipation. The Pratyekas were eminent men; they could attain *nirvāṇa* by their own efforts, without the help of Buddha.

Buddhism contained in this state till the rise of Mahāyāna. The Mahāyāna dismissed the previous theories. They claimed that they could not only attain the *nirvāṇa* but could also help others to attain *nirvāṇa*.

Mahāyāna is of two kinds — Pāramitāyāna and Mantrayāna. Pāramitāyāna is explained by the theories either Sautrāntika (Sarvāstivāda), Yogācāra (Vijñānavāda) or Mādhyamīka (Śūnyavāda). Mantrayāna is explained by the theories of Yogācāra and Mādhyamika.[9] Thus, Mantrayāna commences with the most abstruse theories of Śūnyavāda and Vijñānvāda. The Mantrayāna concerns itself with *mantra* and *yantra*. It believes that certain special mystic forces are generated by reciting words in a certain manner and that they can help one to obtain whatsoever one desires including emancipation.[10]

Belief in *mantra* or in the mysterious power of the sound is a social heritage with the Indian masses from the past. Such beliefs in various forms are to be found in early buddhism also. Worship of *stūpa*, reverence for the mystic *bodhimaṇḍala* or the circle round the famous tree beneath which Buddha attained his *bodhi* were popular features also of early Buddhism.[11] The postures and gestures of Lord Buddha were also held mystically significant. These are elements in early Buddhism which no doubt paved the path for the propagation of *mantra*, *mudrā*, and *maṇḍala* elements in Tāntric Buddhism, but gradually the sexo-yogic practice also began to be referred to. Once esoterism could find admission into the Buddhist fold, all sorts or popular beliefs and practices began

9. *Advayavajra Saṁgraha*, p. 14.
10. T.N. Mishra, *Impact of Tantra on Religion and Art*, p. 83.
11. It has often been assured in the Buddhist Tantra that in response to the muttering of these *bīja-mantras*, the ultimate void (*śūnyatā*) will transform herself into the particular form of God or Goddess and confer infinite benefit on the reciter. The kind of belief in a syllable representing a god or a goddess is a very old belief from the time of Āraṇyakas and the Upaniṣads. Thus, the *mantras* are taken only as a help for the realisation of the absolute void-nature of the universe. As the *mantra* element contains all the secrecy of the potency of sound, the *mudrā* element contains the secrecy of touch as associated with the potency of the physiological system. With the *mantra* and *mudrā*, the element of *maṇḍala* or describing the mystic circles was also introduced.

appearing in it. The Tāntric rituals, generally known as *abhicāra*, gradually made their way into it, and the five *makāras* (*pañca-makāras*) also found place in Buddhist esotericism. The aim of these practices is not the fulfilment of desire; these practices are said to be undertaken only for attainment of the *bodhicitta*, i.e., for the realisation of perfect knowledge or for the attainment of the final state of supreme bliss, and for the upliftment of all beings. This composit system of Tantrism with the introduction of sexo-yogic practice came to be known by the name of Vajrayāna or the Adamantine Path. The meaning of Śūnyayāna is the '*śūnya* vehicle'. *Śūnya* is used in a special sense to represent *vajra*. Vajrayāna was based on Śūnyavāda, — not the *śūnya* of the Mādhyamikas but the *śūnya* of the Vajrayānists with the three elements, *śūnya*, *vijñāna*, and *mahāsukha*. Undoubtedly, it can be said that Buddhist Tantra belongs to Mahāyāna theories. This Tantra was a development of Yogācāra which was inspired by the Śūnyavāda of Mādhyamika. Vajrayāna marks a step in advance even of the Yogācāra thought. The Mahāyāna in the opinion of the Vajrayānists is co-extensive with what they called *dharma* which they considered as eternal and to which was given a more important place in Buddhism; then it was assigned to Buddha himself.

The word *vajrayāna* is characterised as 'the path which leads to perfect enlightenment, wherein *śūnya* is used in a special sense to represent *vajra* (the thunderbolt) — *śūnyatā* (vacuity) is designated as *vajra* because it is firm and sound, and cannot be changed, cannot be pierced, cannot be penetrated, cannot be burnt, and cannot be destroyed. The Vajrayānists refer to *śūnya* in all their writings, but this is not the *śūnya* of the Mādhyamikas about which neither existence nor non-existence nor a combination of the two nor a negation of the two can be predicted. To the Mādhyamikas both the subject and the object are *śūnya* in essence; there is no reality either of the mind or of the external world. Obviously, this is a position which was not agreeable to the Vajrayānists because to them a positive aspect in the *śūnya* was absolutely necessary. Yogācāra or Vijñānavāda goes a little further and the view of Vijñānavāda as formulated by the school is that when emancipation is obtained, it does not become *śūnya*, but turn into eternal consciousness. Vajrayāna, on the other hand, is defined as the "Path which leads to perfect enlightenment".

In Vajrayāna, the easy methods leading to happiness in this world were held out to the people. Easy paths leading to salvation were shown. The disciplinary regulations gradually slackned down one after another and ultimately, when Vajrayānists gained much in power, a general revolution was declared against the Mahāyāna orthodoxy, as it was powerless to fight the growing disorder amongst the Tāntrics.

The followers of Vajrayāna were, however, conscious that they were doing something which was against religion and morality and in order to justify their action, they took shelter under the theory of *karuṇā* and held that there was nothing that could not be done by one who had sacrificed everything for the emancipation of the world. This idea of *karuṇā* is unique in the history of any religion, and Buddhism can very well be proud of this one single conception. But this idea was too much for them. They could neither negate it, nor practise it, nor realise the importance. The result was that the vow to emancipate the whole world was turned into a mere convention, and what is worst, the Vajrayānists took shelter under its cover and found in it an excuse for committing acts of great sin and immorality.

A singular peculiarity that marks out Vajrayāna is that it considered everything as *vajra*. And the most outstanding feature of Vajrayāna is the identification of the ultimate reality with the conception of a Lord Supreme (*bhagavān*) as Vajrasattva, also called Vajradhara. This Vajrasattva is not merely of the nature of the *śūnyatā*, but is as well the non-dual of *śūnyatā* and *karuṇā*. He is thus the being of infinite wisdom and universal compassion. Hence, it is that Vajrasattva is often identified with the *bodhicitta*.[12] He who realises Vajrasattva becomes himself Vajrasattva. To realise Vajrasattva is to bring home to one's mind that all existence is nothing but *śūnyatā* in its pure nature, and as soon as

12. In the *Prajñopāya-viniścayasiddhi*, it is said that the Lord is of the nature of all existence in the form of *bodhicitta*, he is the Lord, the holder of the thunder, and this self verily is God.

one attains to this knowledge, one becomes Vajrasattva.[13] The supreme deity Vajrasattva is often found in the Buddhist Tantra conceived exactly in the manner of the Upaniṣadic *Brahman*. It is often spoken of as the ultimate reality in the form of *bodhicitta*. The Mahāyānic idea of *bodhicitta* also underwent a change beyond recognition in esoteric Buddhism. Originally, it was conceived as the mental state in which there is nothing but a strong resolution for the attainment of perfect wisdom (*bodhi*) combined with the emotion of universal compassion. Thus, *bodhicitta* presupposes two elements in *citta*, viz., *śūnyatā* (i.e., the knowledge of things as pure void) and *karuṇā* (universal compassion). In the practice of Vajrayāna, *bodhicitta* is conceived as the extremely blissful state of mind produced through the sexo-yogic practice. In yogic practices, the union of the seed and the ovum is also known as *bodhicitta* and it has been held that in the process of production this *bodhicitta* acquires the nature of five elements, viz., earth, water, fire, air, and ether, and thus, it stands as the ultimate substance of the universe.

The Vajrayāna conception of the *bodhicitta* appears to be the same as advocated in Yogācāra, the idea of which can be gained by a reference to the *tattva-saṁgraha*. The *bodhicitta* is like a continuous stream of consciousness which changes every moment, the consciousness of the previous moment giving rise to or causing the consciousness of the succeeding moment. The chain of momentary consciousness which is without a beginning or an end, operating in unison with the all powerful force leads it either to degradation or the emancipation accordingly as the actions done are good or bad. The Vajrayānist's conception is the same and it defines *bodhicitta* as one where *śūnya* and *karuṇā* (compassion) work in unison. In the eye of a Vajrayānist the external world has much the same significance as it appears in Yogācāra.

---

13. S.B. Dasgupta, *Introduction to Tāntric Buddhism*, pp. 91-3. He is also called the *mahāsattva* as he is full of the bliss of infinite knowledge, and he is always engaged in the right method of religious observance (*samaya*), he is called the *samaya-sattva* — as he is eternally associated with disciplinary practices for the attainment of wisdom, he is called *bodhisattva*, and as associated with perfect wisdom, he is called *jñāna-sattva*.

Vajrayānists hold that external objects have no greater reality than dream, and their reality cannot be proved by reason.

The pantheon of the Buddhists is extraordinarily extensive and varied in character. The Vajrasattva is the Primal Enlightened one, the Ādi-Buddha. This Lord possesses five kinds of knowledge which are like five attributes of the Lord. From these five kinds of meditation (*dhȳana*) and from these five kinds of *dhyāna* emanate five deities. Who are known as the five *dhyānī* Buddhas. The Tāntric Buddhists develop the theory of the five *dhyānī* Buddhas. The Buddhists believe that the world is composed of five cosmic elements (*skandhas*). The five elements are form (*rūpa*-material element), sensation (*vedanā* = feeling), name (*saṁjñā* = conceptual knowledge), confirmation (*saṁskāra* = synthetic compound, mental states), and consciousness (*vijñāna*). These elements are eternal cosmic forces and are without a beginning or an end. These cosmic forces are defined in Vajrayāna as the five *dhyānī* Buddhas. In course of time, they were regarded as the five primordial gods responsible for this diversified creation, and thus Vajrayāna took a polytheistic form, although polytheism can hardly apply to a system which considers *śūnya* as the one, indivisible and ultimate reality. But so long as form could not be given to *śūnya* as an anthropomorphic deity, the system of five *dhyānī* Buddhas certainly had the flavour of polytheism. The priests and the Vajrayāna authors were conscious of this shortcoming, especially in view of the fact that all the six Hindu systems of philosophy tended to develop a highly monistic philosophy. They tried at first to cure this defect by the theory of the *kulas* (families), and *kuleśas* (lords of families), of gods and men, and thus, divided everything into five groups. For each group, a particular *dhyānī* Buddha becomes the *kuleśa* or the primordial Lord, all other groups taking their origin from him. Another grand conception of the Vajrayāna Buddhism is the theory of the highest god Vajradhara, also called Ādi-Buddha, the primordial monotheistic god who is the embodiment of *śunya* to whom even the *dhyānī* Buddhas owe their origin. The special Tantra dedicated to Ādi-Buddha is the Kālacakra Tantra which appears to be the original Tantra in which the doctrine of Ādi-Buddha was for the first time included. The five *dhyānī* Buddhas are the progenitors of the five *kula*s or families of deities, and communities worshipping them were known as the *kaulasa*, and the process of worship was called *kulācāra* or family conduct. These *dhyānī* Buddhas further spilt themselves up in the form of *bodhisattva* and their female principles who are responsible for creating everything found in existence. The forms of deities are nothing but the gross forms of the different sounds, and thus, the connection of the *mantra* with the deity established. These *dhyānī* Buddhas who are the embodiments of the five *skandha*s or primordial elements are the progenitors of the five families of deities constituting the whole of the Buddhist pantheon.

The *dhyānī* Buddhas are a peculiar kind of Buddha who are not required to pass through the stage of a *bodhisattva*. They were never anything less than a Buddha. They are always engaged in peaceful meditation, and they voluntarily abstain themselves from the act of creation. To create is the work of their emancipation, the Divine *bodhisattva*. The *dhyānī* Buddhas might have owed their origin to the theory of the eternity of the five senses.

This pantheon of the five *dhyānī* Buddhas seems to have evolved in later Buddhism with some influence from the Sāṁkhya philosophy. The five *skandha*s of the Buddhist were mixed up with the *pañca-bhūta* (five material elements) of the Sāṁkhya, viz., earth (*kṣiti*), water (*āp*), fire (*tejas*), air (*marut*) and ether (*vyoma*). These five material elements, together with the five sense-organs, proceed, according to the Sāṁkhya, from five *tanmātra*s (potential elements) or generic essences of sound, touch, colour, taste, and smell. The five *tanmātra*s remind us of the five kinds of knowledge of the Primal Lord which are the five attributes of the Lord, and from these five attributes of knowledge follow the five kinds of *dhyāna*s, from which proceed five *dhyānī* Buddhas, who are the generic essences of the five *skandha*s.

In the Tāntric literature these five *dhyānī* Buddhas are described with their divine consorts (*śakti*s), with particular colour, crest, posture (*mudrā*), and *vāhana*. They are associated with a particular family (*kula*), five sense-organs, etc. These five *dhyānī* Buddhas are also called the five *tathāgatas*. The marking of the first four *tathāgatas* by the miniature of Akṣobhya implies that the first four *skandhas* are nothing but modes and modifications of consciousness; they are the constructions from the consciousness. Pure consciousness which is absolutely free from the notions of *grāhya* and *grāhaka* is the ultimate reality, and this ultimate principle of voidness is the Vajrasattva, and, therefore, even Akṣobhya is marked by the miniature figure of Vajrasattva.

This Vajrasattva is not merely of the nature of *śūnyatā*. It is a non-dual state of *śūnyatā* and *karuṇā*; to imply that the void-consciousness is also of the nature of an identity of both *śūnyatā* and *karuṇā*. Akṣobhya is marked by the Vajrasattva. Thus, the Vajrasattva is identified by the *bodhicitta*. It is said that when *prajñā* or *śūnyatā*-knowledge commingles with universal compassion, there remains no thinker, no thinkable, no thought. This is the state of non-duality, this is called the *bodhicitta*, this is truth, this is Vajrasattva — the perfectly enlightened one (*sambuddha*), this is perfect wisdom. This Vajrasattva (Vajradhara) is also described in Tantras with his consort. This Vajrasattva, the Lord Supreme of the Tāntric Buddhists, is found in the Buddhist Tantras bearing many other names of which the most important are Hevajra and Heruka.

Within the fold of Vajrayāna there arose a school known as Kālacakrayāna, which should not be regarded as a separate school of Tāntric Buddhism distinct from Vajrayāna or the Kālacakrayāna, seems to be later development of the Vajrayāna. It concerns itself with the *yoga-tantra* and *anuttarayoga-tantra* and incorporates the doctrines of the Sahajayāna also. The Supreme Deity in this school is called the Lord Śrī Kālacakra.[14] *Kāla* means the ultimate immutable knowledge (*prajñā*)

14. According to *Kālacakra-tantra*, Kālacakra, a deity and an embodiment of *śūnyatā* and *karuṇā* (compassion), is embraced by the goddess, Prajñā, and represents the philosophical conception of *advaya* or non-duality. He is regarded as the Ādi-Buddha (the progenitor even of the Buddha), that is to say, the *dhyānī* Buddha. One's own body in which the whole world is manifest, has a resemblance to the doctrines of Sahajyāna and Nāthism and this makes it probable that the Kālacakrayāna is embodied in the teachings of the Vajrayāna, Sahajayāna, and Nāthism. T.N. Mishra, *Impact of Tantra on Religion and Art*, p. 83.

or the state of *śūnyatā*, while the *cakra* means the cycle of the world process, or the body of the Lord containing the potency of the existence of the universe, which is just the principle of *upāya*. Therefore, *kālacakra*[15] implies the absolutely unified principle of *prajñā* and *upāya*, and he is thus *bodhicitta*. In some Tantras he is characterised as *śūnyata* and *karuṇā* unified, as the non-dual Lord, and as embracing *prajñā*. There is, therefore, no essential difference between the two conceptions of Kālacakra and Vajrasattva. As to other matters also, the principle and method are the same both in Kālacakrayāna and Vajrayāna. One distinctive feature is the stress on time which is the common meaning of the term *kāla*. Time, with all its divisions and sub-divisions (moment, hour, day, night, week, fortnight, month and year) dwells within one's body, in which lies the whole universe with all its animate and inanimate objects. And time with its divisions is caused by, or is the production of, the vital winds (*vāyus*) that remain diffused throughout the entire nervous system of one's body. One who can control the vital winds in the nerves by yogic practices, thereby puts oneself above all influence of the whirls of time which is the root cause of all miseries including decay and destruction.

The Vajrayāna and Kālacakrayāna completed the evolution of Buddhism in India. Hīnayāna was practically dislodged by Mahāyāna; Mahāyāna, too, in its turn, was to a considerable extent eclipsed by Vajrayāna, which 'revolted against both the monasticism and scholasticism of Hīnayāna Buddhism and the intellectual pedantry of the Mahāyānists, and now began to make its triumphant headway.[16]

15. The word *kālacakra* means the wheel of time or the circle of time. In another word *kāla* means time, death, and destruction. The *kālacakra* is the wheel of destruction, and Kālacakrayāna means the vehicle for protection from the wheel of destruction. The 6th chapter of *Tantrāloka* of Abhinavagupta has discussed the theory of *kālacakra*, and is devoted to the exposition of the doctrine of *kāla* (time), and the process of keeping oneself above the influence of time. Every syllable of the word *kālacakra* is said to be pregnant with a meaning, the syllable *ka* indicates unruffled causality in which there should be the final absorption as is indicated by the syllable *la*, *ca* indicate unsteady mind, and *kra* means the series of events or the process.

16. Shashi Bhushan Dasgupta, *Obscure Religious Cults*, p. 86.

After the demise of Lord Buddha, the spirit of revolution, which served as the very kernel of all Buddhistic thought and religion, faded as a result of slow but continuous friction with Hindu thoughts and practices. As a result, there seems to have developed a spirit of compromise by which the concept of Tantrism entered Buddhism, giving rise to a composite religion known as Tāntric Buddhism or Sahajīya Buddhism. Sahajīya Buddhism developed a theology of their own which is substantially different from the philosophy and religion of canonical Buddhism.

The Sahajīya School is an offshoot of Vajrayāna. There is no exclusive literature belonging to Sahajayāna. On the other hand, the Sahajīya poets of the *dohās* and songs recognise the well-known text of Vajrayāna as their authority. The exponents of the Sahaja school put the whole emphasis on their protest against the formalities of life and religion. For truth, they affirmed, was a matter of intuition and could never be attained by these artificial and unnatural means. To that end one must proceed through the natural way, which lies not in discarding the inborn propensities of human beings and the total annihilation of the sex passion, but in sublimating the same. In the nature of man, hunger and sex are recognised as the most primitive and fundamental propensities. Other religions prescribed strict rules for their suppression, which is absolutely unnatural. The Sahajīyas would never prescribe any unnatural strain on human nature, but would take human nature itself as the best help for realising the truth. It is for this reason that this path has always been described as the easiest and most natural. This makes the position of the Sahajīyas distinct from that of the Vajrayānists in general. It will be totally wrong to suppose that the question of moral discipline was in any way less emphasised in the Sahajīya school than in other schools of religion. It is Sahajayāna; its aim is to realise the ultimate innate nature (*sahaja*) of the self as well as of the *dharma*, and it is Sahajayāna that instead of suppressing, and thereby, inflicting undue strain on the human nature, it makes man realise the truth in the most natural way. The path was one of *yoga* practices, for the process of *yoga*, according to their way of thinking, takes its rise from one's sex impulses. Our sex-passions are part and parcel of our nature; therefore, *yogīs* transform this sex passion into a yogic process for realising truth.

All the important Tāntric sects had one common goal, the attainment of non-duality (*advaya*), also called *sahaja* or *kaula,* the state in which all dualistic knowledge disappears and the *sādhaka* becomes identical with the object of his devotion. For attaining this aim different sects advocated different means ranging from the sexo-yogic techniques of rousing *kuṇḍalinī* to *aghorī* practices. The Sahajiyās were averse to the method of knowing the truth through discursive method and were not in favour of meditation and *mantra*. They protested against the formalities of life and religion and accepted human nature as the best help for realising the truth.[17] Sexual orgies were practised by the Kaulas and Kāpālikas. Attainment of salvation meant becoming like Buddha and Alakhanirañjana. The Buddhist Sahajīyas Nātha-*pathīṣ* believed in *bindu-siddhi* on yogic control of semen (*vīrya*) during the sexual act and gave much attention to the *vāmācāra* rites including *cakra-pūjā*, the worship of living beautiful women, and the practice of a secret form of intercourse where there was no distinction of caste. Thus, it seems that the serious intent in the rigorous path of Tāntric *sādhanā* was lost, leaving behind the belief that only the pursuit of pleasure ultimately led to *mokṣa*.

With the influential concept of Śāktism, the primitive Tāntric rituals, basically sexual in character, made their way into different kinds of religious systems as the highly technical and sophisticated culture of the five *makāras*. The women, flesh, and sexual intercourse came to be regarded as essential pre-conditions for attainment of liberation. The

17. In the Anuśāsana-parva of the *Mahābhārata,* where Bhīṣma is describing to Yudhiṣṭhira the really sacred places of pilgrimage, we find that the mind with the transparent water of purity and truth, when associated with the lake of patience, is the best of all places of pilgrimage. He whose body is washed with water cannot be said to be the really cleansed one. One who has controlled all his senses is the really cleaned one and he is pure within as well as without. To dive into the water of the bliss of Brahma-knowledge in the lake of the pure heart, is the best of all bathing, and it is only he whom the wise recognise to be a real pilgrim. *Mahābhārata*, Anuśāsana-parva.

idea of *yuganaddha* (god in sexual union with goddess), an iconological form by which the Buddha and *bodhisattva* were frequently represented, shows the extent to which the Buddhist were influenced by the Tāntric way of life. The central theme of the two basic works on Tāntric Buddhism deals with the *mudrā*s and *maṇḍala*s which are connected with goddesses and spiritually oriented women who can come from any class of people. The aspirant has to understand that the woman or her generative organ is the source of existence and that sexual functioning is the imitation of the process of creation.

According to the Tāntric view the act of creation is due to the union of the female and male principles, the former being the more important functionary. In Buddhist Tantra these two principles are known as *prajñā* and *upāya* or *śūnya* and *karuṇā*, this is also known as *lalanā* and *rasanā* respectively.[18] The union of *prajñā* and *upāya* is *yuganaddha* or *samarasa*. One who can unite these two principles in oneself can have the highest knowledge and supreme bliss, and become free from the fetters of birth and death. This is the real Buddhahood. In order to have this spiritual experience, man and woman should first realise that they are representatives of *upāya* and *prajñā* respectively and that their physical, mental, and intellectual union alone can bring the experience of the highest truth.[19] Accordingly, man and woman should jointly strive for this secret knowledge, *prajñā* is the female principle, and as such, she is Bhagavatī or the goddess herself. She is known as *vajra kanyā* and *yuvatī*.

---

18. *Prajñā* and *upāya* are also known as *lalanā* and *rasanā*. Which are the names of the two nerves, *iḍā* and *piṅgalā* in the Hindu Tāntric nerves system. That in which the two nerves commingle is called the *avadhūti,* that is known as *suṣumnā* nerve in the Hindu Tantra, and this nerve is regarded as the way to *nirvāṇa*. It has been said that *lalanā* is of the nature of *prajñā* and *rasanā* of *upāya*, and *avadhūti* stays in the middle as the abode of *mahāsukha*. The nerves in the right and left in the microcosm of the body represent the principles of duality. Their separate function which binds one to the world of sufferings must, therefore, be checked by the *yogins* and they must unite with the middle nerve and function conjointly. The middle nerve is, therefore, the middle path which leads to the non-dual state of *sahaja*.

19. Alex Wayman, "Female Energy and Symbolism in the Buddhist Tantra", in *History of Religion*, Vol. II, No. 1, p. 80.

The woman who is to impersonate *prajñā* should preferably be a beautiful maiden. *Prajñā* also denotes the female organ (*bhaga*) as she breaks or obstructs all the afflictions, which is the seat of all happiness, also known as Sukhāvatī. *Upāya*, the male principle, is known as *vajra,* which means the male generative organ. The union of man and woman, of *prajñā* and *upāya*, brings the maximum pleasure in which all mental action is lost and the world around forgotten; only a pleasing experience of non-duality prevails.[20] This is known as the *mahāsukha* (greatest pleasure) or *nirvāṇa*, the *summum-bonum* and real manifestation of *bodhicitta*.

In the Buddhist Tantras the element of *nirvāṇa* is described as incessant bliss (*sukha-maya*), it is the abode of both enjoyment as well as liberation, it is called *mahāsukha*, where there is no change or decrease. It is the seed of all substance, it is the ultimate stage of those who have attained perfection, it is the highest place of the Buddha, and is called the Sukhāvatī (the abode of bliss). *Mahāsukha* is something which has neither existence nor annihilation, it has neither a beginning nor any middle, nor any end; this transcendental supreme bliss is neither the not-self nor the self.

The *sukha* is not possible at all without the body, without body none would even be able to speak of *saukhya*. In the *guhya siddhi* it is said that through the union of the void-elements (*śūnyatā* = *prajñā* = female)

---

20. The highest mental joy that ensues from the coital act is only momentary or ephemeral with the discharge of semen; its normal downward flow when checked and reversed by the *yogī* towards the seat of consciouness in the lotus — the 'return of semen' — marks the emanation of the supreme bliss that is permanent, and the cause of immortality. Thus, it is *śukram* or 'semen virile' that is sometimes described as the supreme bliss. In the *Hevajra-tantra*, the Lord Buddha himself says, "I am existence, I am not existence, I am the Enlightened one or I am enlightened about what things are. My nature is that of *sahaja* bliss and I come at the end of joy of cessation (*virāmā-nanda*). I am the lord with thirty-two marks, the Lord with eighty characteristics. I dwell in the Sukhāvatī of the *bhaga* (vagina) of woman and my form is *śukram* (semen) — without that (i.e., *śukram*) there is no bliss, and without bliss this would not be. Since, one can never be effective without the other, bliss ensues only in union with female divinity." *Hevajratantra*, ed. and tr. by Snellgrov, Vol. I and II, pp. 48-50; T.N. Mishra, *Impact of Tantra on Religion and Art*, pp. 85, 90.

and the thunder (*vajra* = *upāya* = male) the great element is produced in the form of bliss which yields *paramānanda*; after the cessation of *paramānanda* is produced *virāmānanda*, and the supreme bliss that follows *virāmānanda* is of indescribable nature, it is bereft of all the senses, it is the ultimate stage of liberation to the *sādhaka*s, the pure transcendental non-substantial *bodhicitta*. The bliss that is produced through some cause, itself destroys the cause of *saṁsāra*. The nature of *mahāsukha* cannot be realised through the theories of the void and all other false constructions. Through the purification of *prajñā* and *upāya*, it is revealed that *mahāsukha* is the one non-dual knowledge. When *prajñā* and *upāya* are combined together in oneness, the non-dual knowledge is produced which is *mahāsukha*.

The Sahajayāna holds that the pleasure that is realised through the discharge of matter is much lower, than the bliss that can be realised through the control of this matter, i.e., by checking its downward flow through subtle yogic processes and by giving it an upward flow so as to make it reach the lotus situated in the cerebrum region (*uṣṇīśa-kamala*, corresponding to the *sahasrāra-padma* of the Hindu Tantra) and to make it steady there. The bliss resulting from the steadiness of the matter is the *mahāsukha*. But in the popular way, we often find semen-virile described as *mahāsukha*, and it is Lord Buddha himself. Lord Buddha dwells in the elysium of Sukhāvatī (the abode of bliss). Here, the female organ is described as the Sukhāvatī where the Lord Mahāsukha dwells in his own nature as supreme bliss.[22]

---

21. *Yuganaddha* is also described as the non-dual state and is identified with the *bodhicitta*, and it is defined as a state of absolute non-duality marked by the absence of notions like worldly process and cessation of that process (*nivṛtti*), adherence (*saṁkleśa*) and distinction (*vyavadhāna*), and perceivable and perceiver (*grāhya* and *grāhaka*). H.V. Guenther, *Yuganānddha*.

22. In the *Hevajra-tantra* we find that the Lord (*bhagavān*) is explaining his own nature to the *bodhisattva* Vajragarbha. "I am Buddha (perfectly enlightened one) as I have perfect knowledge about things, fools can never know anything of me. I dwell in the *sukhāvatī* of the vagina of the good thunder-woman (*śad-vajra-yoṣit*) which is of the form of letter *e*, and which is the abode of the jewels of the Buddha. I am the world and everything belongs to the world. I am of the nature of the *sahaja*-bliss; I am *paramānanda* as well as *virāmānanda*, etc.; I

→

This *sahaja* bliss (*mahāsukha*) is not to be misunderstood as gross sex pleasure. It is the subtlest and the highest state of becoming that could only be reached by experiencing distinct stages (momentary of bliss in an ascending order). It demarcates the *cakra*s or centres of consciousness at different planes or levels of anthropomorphic personality. The *cakra*s along with their particular 'flavour' of joys transform the individual personality stage by stage into cosmic existence or selfless immortality.

In the Tantras, we find that the world proceeds from the bliss which is the cessation of all duality and is the nature of ultimate reality. It has been said that bliss (*ānanda*) is to be known as Brahma, from bliss proceeds all the objects, through bliss they live, and in bliss do they return and merge.[23] We find an echo of the same truth in the utterances of the Sahajīyas, who say that all the beings are born in *sahaja*, they live in *sahaja* and again return to *sahaja*. The *sahaja* is the *rasa*, the supreme emotion of love, the quintessence in everybody. It is the primordial emotion, it is *kāma* and from *kāma* proceeds everything. There is sometimes the tendency of explaining the two stages of *sahaja* (i.e., *rasa* and *rati*) under the imagery of seed and ovum and the cosmos as following from their union, just as it is explained in the texts of the Tāntric and Buddhist Sahajīya Schools. Both the self and the non-self being thus the product of *sahaja* are homogeneous in their ultimate nature, and it is, therefore, that the realisation of the nature of the self through the culture of love leads also to the realisation of the ultimate nature of the non-self.

The final aim in all such cases was the attainment of an infinitely

---

→ am faith, like a light in the darkness; I dwell in the *sukhāvatī* of the vagina of the female in the name of semen." It is further said, "Without him (semen) there is no bliss, and again without bliss he cannot be. As he can never be related, there is no other source of realising him except the divine esoteric practice." It is, therefore, said that Buddha (in the form of semen) is neither existence nor non-existence, in spite of having face and form he is formless in the nature of supreme bliss. *Hevajra-tantra*, MS 36(A), 36(B), and *Royal Asiatic Society of Bengal*, No. 4854, p. 47(A).

23. *Taittirīyopaniṣad*, III.6.

blissful state of arrest (*samādhi*), either purely through the a psycho-physiological process of *yoga* or through the absorbing emotion of love, strictly disciplined and intensified through practice of *yoga*. Intense human love or sexual pleasure, thus transformed beyond recognition, has the capacity to produce a supreme state of arrest. In a unique flow of intensely blissful realisation, uninterrupted by the notions of subjectivity and objectivity, then dawns an infinite oneness in the mind, which is said to be a state of unity of emotion (*samarasa*). All the subjective and objective disturbances of the mind are absolutely lost in a supreme realisation of bliss, and in that state we attain our true self, which is *sahaja*.[24] To judge this state of *samarasa* or *sahaja* as a pure state of *samādhi*, a *sādhaka* practises *yoga* in the plane of mind (*citta-bhūmi*). According to the view of the Sahajīyas the flow of bliss must be made to march upwards through the different *kāya*s, and finally reach the region of *sahaja-kāya*. In the process of upward march, the bliss first produced goes on acquiring a higher nature and when it reaches the *sahaja-kāya* or *uṣṇīśa-kamala* it becomes *mahāsukha*, where all kinds of duality vanish in a unique realisation of supreme bliss.

A dominant feature of Sahajayāna is its stress on the middle path avoiding the opposite extremes of views. With the idea of *advaya* (*yuganaddha*), the final state is that where all kinds of duality are absorbed in a principle of non-duality. The nerves in the right and the left in the microcosm of the body represent the principles of duality; their separate functions which bind one to the world of sufferings must, therefore, be checked by the *yogin*s, and they must unite with the middle nerve and function them conjointly. The middle nerve is, therefore, the middle path which leads to the non-dual state of *sahaja*.

The flow of *bodhicitta* must be regulated along the middle nerve,

---

24. In the Upaniṣad, realisation of self has been compared to the transcendental realisation of bliss arising through the deep embrace of loving women. Thus, it is said, "As, when deeply embraced by the dear woman, one knows neither anything external nor anything internal — so also a man deeply embraced by the self (*ātman*) through perfect knowledge knows neither anything external nor anything internal." *Bṛhadāraṇyaka Upaniṣad*, IV.3.2.1.

and this is the most important, and at the same time the most difficult part of *sādhanā*, and it is for this reason that we find repeated warnings to the novice to take practical suggestions from a preceptor at this stage. If the flow of *bodhi-citta* moves either left or right, the whole thing is spoiled. The *apāna* wind, has always a downward motion; the *prāṇa* an upward motion; therefore, the *yogin* should arrest the course of both the *prāṇa* and the *apāna*, and then make them flow the middle nerve and with this flow of vital wind within the middle nerve, the *bodhi* will also flow upward and reach the *uṣṇīśa-kamala*, and thereby, *mahāsukha* will be produced. The *bodhicitta* should then be made steady by making steady the breath, and this state of *yoga* is the ultimate stage for the *yogin*. In this production of the *bodhicitta*, four stages associated with four *cakra*s (lotuses) are distinctly marked, and on the basis of the four stages, we find mention of four *mudrā*s (viz., *karma-mudrā*, *dharma-mudrā*, *mahā-mudrā*, and *samaya-mudrā*), which are the four stages of *yoga*. There are four mental states called the four moments (viz., *vicitra*, *vipāka*, *vimarda*, and *vilakṣaṇa*),[25] and four kinds of bliss (viz., *ānanda*, *paramānanda*, *virāmānanda*, and *sahajānanda*). *Ānanda* is the bliss when the *bodhicitta* is in the *nirmāṇa-cakra*, *paramānanda* in the *dharma-cakra*, *viramānanda* in the *saṁbhoga-cakra*, and *sahajānanda* is more intense. *Virāmānanda* means the detachment from the worldly pleasure, and *sahajānanda* is the final bliss.[26]

25. *Hevajra-tantra*, M.S.L.39(A).
26. *Śrī-Kālacakra-tantra*, M.S.L. 57(A).

    Hevajra-tantra, M.S.L., 27(A).

    In the Sekoddiśa Ṭīkā, we find that *ānanda* is the pleasure of passion which disturbs the mind; *paramānanda* is the realisation of full bliss when the *bodhicitta* reaches the forehead; the next stage is the stage of *virāmānanda* when nectar oozes from the moon in the forehead. Even in this stage of *virāmānanda*, the *sādhaka* retains his consciousness of egohood, i.e., the realisation of the bliss in this stage is associated with some sort of self-consciousness, but this self-consciousness is totally lost in the stage of *sahajānanda* where the knower and the knowable are lost in the oneness of perfect bliss. Of the sixteen digits of the moon the first five represent *ānanda*, up to the tenth is *paramānanda*, up to the fifteenth is *virāmānanda*, and the sixteenth represents *sahajānanda*. Again, corresponding to the four stages, viz., the state of wakefulness (*jāgrata*), dream (*svapna*), deep sleep (*suṣupta*), and →

Connected with the yogic practice of the Sahajīya Buddhists is the conception of the female force. This *yoginī* (*sahaja-sundarī*) should not be confused with the woman of flesh and blood, associated with the actual yogic practices; she is but an internal force of the nature of *śūnyatā* (vacuity) or *nirātmā* (essencelessness) and the great bliss residing in different pleasures in different stages of yogic practice. In the *Sādhana-mālā*, we find that *mahā-mudrā* resides in the naval, and she is produced of *mahāsukha*, and for intense scorch, she is described as of the nature of fire. She is of the nature of the first vowel, she is taken to be the wisdom by the Buddhas, she remains pervading the three elements (*tri-dhātu*), and is never known by lay people (*pr̥thag-jana*).[27]

It is clear that the production of *bodhicitta* and its upward march through the different *kāya*s to the *uṣṇīśa-kamala* to be transformed into *mahāsukha* is closely associated with the question of raising the *śakti* from the lowest pole of phenomenalism to the highest pole of absolute truth. When *śakti* reaches the *sahaja-kāya,* she becomes *śūnyatā* herself, and our perfected *citta* becomes the Lord Vajrasattva; real *mahāsukha* follows only when this *śūnyatā* is united in the *sahaja-kāya* with the Vajrasattva.

The fundamental side of Tantra, the most important thing, is the stress laid on the body as the medium in which truth can be realised. The Tāntric maxim recognises that the body is the epitome of the universe, and this is also the basis of Medical Sciences; it rests on the assumption that the elements forming the body cannot be dissociated from environmental elements and that by applying the laws, which govern the latter, the former may be brought into order. For the religious aspirant in the Tantra, there is nothing apart from the body, the functioning of which is considered to belong to the same order as cosmic functioning. The different metaphysical systems deal with the nature of

---

→ the fourth or final state (*turīya*), we have four elements viz., body (*kāya*), speech (*vāk*), mind (*citta*), and knowledge (*jñāna*); we have four kinds of bliss in each of these states, and thus the actual number of bliss becomes sixteen in all. — G.O.S., pp. 26-7.

27. *Sādhana-Mālā*, Vol. II, p. 448 (G.O.S.).

reality and the philosophic method for its apprehension; but, Tantra lays stress on the practical method for realising that reality. This practical aspect of *sādhanā* is the essential part of Tantra. Now, in this practical aspect, the whole of Tāntric *sādhanā* is based on the cardinal belief that the truth is to be realised in and through the body.

The belief of the *tāntrikas* is that the ultimate truth is not an abstract principle transcending the universe but is immanent in it, and that the human body is not merely a thing in the universe, the microcosm exists in relation to the macrocosm. Therefore, there is nothing in the universe which is not in the body of man. There is perfect parallelism between the physical process of the universe and the biological processes in the body of man; with this idea, the Tantra tries to locate sun, moon, stars, the mountains, islands, rivers, and seas of the external world within the human body. The time element of the universe in all its phases of day and night, month and year, have been explained with reference to the course of the vital wind (*prāṇa* and *apāna*). The human body, with its physical structure and biological processes, represents the manifestation of the same energy which is at play in the structure and processes vast cosmos. The *sādhaka* should concentrate his attention on himself and realise the truth within, with the clear conviction that the truth that is realised within is the truth that pervades the universe without.

According to *yogī* (*haṭha-yogī*), the body is not only the abode of truth, but is the best medium for realising the truth. Different plexuses (lotuses or *cakras*), nerves, and nerve-centres represent different *tattvas* (essential principles), but the *tattvas* represented by them lie latent until they are made potent through proper yogic culture and control.[28] Through this,

28. The centre of power in the human body is not an innovation of the Tāntric. It has its root in the cosmic law of evolution, and is revealed to mankind for their salvation. The centre of power is the cause from which the five sheaths arise. These are sheath of food (*annamaya- kośa*), the sheath of life (*prāṇamaya-kośa*), the sheath of lower mind (*manomaya-kośa*), the sheath of higher mind (*vijñānamaya kośa*), and the sheath of bliss (*ānandamaya-kośa*). The *ānandamaya-kośa* arises from the elements, earth, water, and fire. Earth and water produce food, which is assimilated by fire and converted into substance which forms the body it nourishes. Earth, water, and fire are the presiding →

the physical system may be transformed into a perfect instrument for reflecting the truth.

The physiological analysis of the nerves and the 'lotuses' will help us in understanding the yogic process of Tāntric Buddhism. The analysis of the physical system starts with the spinal cord, widely known as the *merudaṇḍa* (the bone from the bottom of the back up to the medulla oblongata). The name *merundaṇḍa* is significant, it has been said that in the form of the skeleton-bone the great mountain Sumeru remains in the body. This spinal column is compared to the mountain. According to the Buddhist Tantra, there are four plexuses. The first is the lumber plexus situated in the naval region, the second is the cardiac plexus in the heart, the third is the laryngeal and pharyngeal plexus at the junction of the spinal cord and the medulla oblongata, and the last and most important is the cerebral plexus called the *uṣṇīśa-kamala* (in Hindu Tantra known as *sahasarāra*).

Buddhist Tantra speaks of three nerve cycles symbolising the three bodies of Budda — *dharma*, *saṁbhoga*, and *rūpa* or *nirmāṇa*. An additional nerve cycle is *uṣṇīśa-kamala* in the central region which is the symbol of the Buddha's *vajra-kāya* or *sahaja-kāya* and which corresponds to the Śākta concept of *sahasrāra*. Below this, around the neck is *saṁbhoga-cakra*, near the heart is *dhama-cakra,* and near the naval is

→ elements in *mūlādhāra*, *svādhiṣṭhāna*, and *maṇipūra* centres respectively. They become the objects of concentration in the first place, as by awakening the *kula-kuṇḍalinī*; the *sādhaka* first meets *mūlādhāra*, then *svādhiṣṭhāna,* and then *maṇipūra*. The *prāṇamaya-kośa* arises from *anāhata* and *viśuddha* centres in which vital air and space (ether) respectively reside. It includes the ten sense which form the vital breath. It is a subtle form of manifestation. *The manomaya kośa* is evolved from the *ājñā-cakra*, which is the centre of the mind. The mind is the faculty which discriminates between the physical sensations of the five perceptive senses. The *vijñānamaya kośa* arises from the *bindu* and *nāda*. It directly reflects the intelligence (*buddhi*) of the material body (*kāraṇa-śarīra*) or the principles of five senses of man and undifferentiated nature (*prakṛti*). In *sahasrāra*, there is *ānandamaya-kośa*.

The different kinds of energy that we find working in nature are different expressions of one great energy. This is, in scientific terminology, known as correlation of forces.

— T.N. Mishra, *Impact of Tantra on Religion and Art*, pp. 50-1.

nirmāṇa-cakra. There are innumerable nerves within the body. Of these, three are most important: two, symbolising *prajñā* and *upāya*, are on the either side of the spinal cord, and the third is known as *sahaja* or *avadhūti*. Like the *kuṇḍalinī-śakti* of the Śākta Tantra, the Buddhist Tantra speaks of a female energy having the force of fire which resides in *nirmāṇa-cakra*, and is known as *cāṇḍālī*. This *cāṇḍālī* being accelerated, it kindles the *dharma* and *saṁbhoga-cakra*, and ultimately reaches the *uṣṇīśa-kamala*, the highest cerebral region, and then returns to its own place.[29]

In the Buddhist Tantra, the nerve *lalanā* (*āli*) starts from the neck and enters the naval region from the left side, and from the naval again starts the *rasanā* (*kāli*) and enters the neck from the right. Within these two and passing through the lotus in the heart is the *avadhūti*, through which flows the *bodhi-citta*, and this *avadhūtikā* leads to the *sahaja* bliss, and it itself is often described as the *sahaja*-bliss.

As a man versed in the science of poison knows poison as poison and then swallows some quantity of it and yet he never falls swooning thereby, on the other hand, becomes cured of diseases, so also is the case with an expert *yogin*, who attains liberation through enjoyment. The *citta* or mind being the ultimate ground of all creation, the nature of the *citta* will determine the nature of all appearance in the form of action; and so, all actions done with a pure mind cannot but be pure even if sex-relation is involved in them. All the notions of right and wrong are created by the *citta*, and it is through the *citta* again that they are all destroyed. It should be remembered that whenever *citta* clings to the objects of desire, the ultimate nature of the self can be realised through the enjoyment of the worldly objects, only then the ultimate nature of the world is realised as the vacuity through the instructions of the preceptor, and in such a state there reins no difference between the world and the vacuity as there is no difference between the water of a river and its waves. Profound and secret are the ways of this cult, who can say anything and who can hear? Who is really engaged in this cult? This path is just like an underground passage of water.

29. Nagendra Nath Upadhyaya, *Tantric Bauddha Sādhanā aur Sāhitya,* pp. 12-14; S.B. Dasgupta, *An Introduction to Tantric Buddhism,* p. 77.

4

Nātha Cult

THE esoteric cult professed by the Kanaphaṭa *yogī* wearing the *kuṇḍala* is known as the Nātha cult.

The Nātha cult is a yogic cult and it seems to represent a particular phase of *siddha* cult of India. This *siddha* cult is a very old religious cult with its main emphasis on a process of *yoga*, that is known as the *kāya-sādhanā* or the culture of body with a view to making it perfect and immutable, and thereby attaining an immortal spiritual life. All the great teachers of this cult generally bear the title of 'Nātha', so this cult is known as Nātha cult. The traditional belief of Nātha is that Ādi-Nātha (Primal Lord) is the first in the list of Nāthas, and all secrets of *yoga* proceed from him. This Ādi-Nātha is none but Lord Śiva, who is also known as Bhūta-Nātha, *bam-bam* is the mystic sound of the Nātha *yogins* as it is of Śiva himself.

Judging from the literary records, the legends and traditions still prevalent among the *yogins* of the Nātha cult is; seems, a Śaivaite Cult: Mahādeva or Śiva being the original teacher of this cult. Wearing *kuṇḍala*, he uses *rudrākṣa*, i.e., rosaries and *tripuṇḍra* of ash on the forehead. *Śivarātrī* is the major festival of this cult. Vaiṣṇava association, Buddhist affiliation and association with Jaina, and other sects are well woven into the complex texture of the Nātha Cult. Śākta elements are also accepted in this cult. This cult (Nātha) was never seriously theistic. The Supreme Being was referred to by the epithets *nirañjana* (speckless), *śūnya* (void), *anādi* (that which has no beginning), and Ādi-Nātha (primal lord).[1] Patañjali, the great exponent or propounder of Yoga, who dealt primarily with the psychological aspect of Yoga, also devoted a full chapter of the *Yogasūtra* to the different kinds of supernatural powers (*vibhūti*s) attainable through concentration of mind on different objects or on different centres of the body. The eight supernatural faculties, viz., *animā* (the power of becoming as small as an atom), *mahimā* (the power of becoming big), *laghimā* (the power of assuming excessive lightness as will), *garimā* (the power of becoming as heavy as one likes), *prāpti* (the power of obtaining everything at will), *prakāmya* (the power of obtaining all objects of pleasure at will), *iśitva* (the power of obtaining supremacy over things), and *vaśitva* (the power of subduing, fascinating, or bewitching) are well-known as the eight powers of Lord Śiva himself, who is the Lord of Yoga.

The idea of a suprenatural power (*siddhi*) is universal in ancient Indian religious systems. Almost all sects attach great importance to Yoga in some form or the other. A *siddha* is one who possesses these powers. The great human teachers who had attained powers through the practice of Yoga, according to the theory, were the eighty-four *siddha*s. All *siddha*s are historical personages and authors of works on their special *sādhanā* (spiritual practice). The general trend of teaching was esoteric, and a qualified teacher (preceptor) was allowed to initiate the disciples in the mysteries. These teachers (*guru*s) were also known as *siddhācārya* and was given an exalted position. The truth that is free from duality was taught by the *guru* and it was believed that nothing was unattainable by him whom the teacher favoured.

Indian religions, from the very beginning of the Vedic time down to the modern era, invariably involve some kind of practice either

1. The Nātha *siddha*s believe that Ādi-Nātha was the first Nātha, the founder of all esoteric science. He is very often equated with Śiva and Vajrasattva.

ceremonial or ritualistic or yogic; the Tantra also lays greatest emphasis on the practical aspect of religion and the practices enjoined in the Tantra are very secret and complex, there is chance of physical or mental aberration at every step. On the one hand, these practices when properly and systematically carried out, may lead a man to the highest spiritual elevation through the realisation of the truth,[2] on the other hand, they may lead a man to the darkest abyss of hell, if these are not very cautiously and methodically carried out with the directions of the experienced *guru*. It is for this reason that most of the Tantras devoted chapters to the selection of a good preceptor and a good disciple. What actually happened, however, was that neither a suitable teacher (*guru*) was available nor an adept underwent the preliminary course of training. Such non-observation of the conditions prescribed in Tantra inevitably led to abuses. It is the teacher who opens the eye of his disciple to the true meaning, and guides him through the dark to the realm of light which is the spiritual kingdom.

---

2. According to the scholars of Tantra, bliss is the nature of the Absolute, which is conceived both positively and negatively. The absolute is realised by us when we realise our self as bliss. The ultimate aim is, therefore, to attain a state of perfect bliss. In all our ordinary experiences of pleasure, we have but a momentary glimpse of the same bliss as constitutes the ultimate nature of our self. But these experiences of pleasure, because of their extremely limited and defiled nature, binds us to a lower plane of life, instead of contributing to an advancement towards self-satisfaction. The *sādhanā* may transform even gross sense-pleasure into the boundless serenity of perfect bliss.

   In our ordinary life we have the experience of the most intense pleasure in our sex-experience. It is carnal passion, sensuous desire which seeks appeasement in the coils of flesh. Sexual union is a sacred Yoga which though involving enjoyment of all the sensual pleasures, gives the ultimate realisation. It is the state of perfect beatitude when the mind has reached the highest aesthetic level and sees the world as a vast ocean of love, wide is the difference between this sex-pleasure and perfect bliss which is the ultimate nature of self and the not self, this distinction can be removed by a total change of perspective and process. The sexo-yogic *sādhanā* of *tāntrikas* is a *sādhanā* for transforming this sex-pleasure into realisation of infinite bliss in which the self and the world around are lost in all-pervading oneness. By knowing it, the path of immortality is opened. The philosophy of life is the reconciliation of different contradictions which paves the way to the absolute.

What was the *sādhanā* in which the *guru* had to initiate his disciple? This *sādhanā* involved the practice of a new form of *yoga*, which evolved in the hands of the *siddhācāryas*. The Tāntric Yoga does not go against nature; it follows the law of nature, which is by itself inclined more towards self-realisation. According to Tāntric Yoga, the *sādhaka* should have a positive attitude. First, it means accepting the worldly desires and objects of enjoyment (*bhoga*), and treating them in such a way as to move towards sublimation. Secondly, it means having the attitude that everything of the world is divine. Hence, we cannot kill the desires, we can only transform or sublimate them. This is the reason why Tantra advocates the *sādhanā* of *kaula-mārga* or *vāma-mārga*. The basic desire (sex-desire) is accepted in Tantra as a current of energy originating from one and the same basic source, *cit-śakti* or *kuṇḍalinī*. The Tantra aims at controlling and regulating these currents so that they flow through sublime channels and yield better results.

The final aim of the Nātha *siddhas* is to attain the state of *parā-mukti* in and through the state of *jīvana-mukti* (liberation) through the attainment of Śivahood or the state of Maheśvara. It is for this reason that in common belief we find great Nātha *siddhas* identified with Śiva (Maheśvara). Immortality is recognised as the quintessence of the ultimate nature of Lord Śiva. The aim of the existence of the cult was the attainment of the state of neutrality (*sahaja*) where there is no birth and death as such. According to the philosophy of the cult, existence and extinction are results of man's desire and cognition; his fetters and mode of release are of his own creation as well. A true *yogī* moves beyond the world of thought, to him activity (*karma*) has no appeal, and salvation (*nirvāṇa*) is meaningless. For the attainment of the state of neutrality, the *yogī*, following the instructions of his *guru* (spiritual teacher), has to check the downward movement of the semen, hold up the truth, and stabilise the mind. These processes are known as *bindu-dhāraṇa*, *citta-nirodha*, and *pavanniścāñcalaya*.[3]

---

3. The fall of semen is considered a great sin. The semen must not be emitted, for otherwise the *yogin* falls under the Law of Time and Death. For checking the flow of semen, the *sādhaka* practices coitus reservations by taking recourse of →

The Nātha *siddhas* called their *sādhanā kāya-sādhanā* (culture of the body) with a view to attaining *kāya-siddhi* (perfection of the body). The porcess has been called as regressive process (*ulṭā-sādhanā*). The *yoga* practices of the Nātha *siddhas* is *ulṭā*, firstly in the sense that it involves yogic processes which give upward motion to the whole biological as well as psychological systems which in their nature possess a downward tendency; and secondly, in the sense that such yogic practice leads the *siddha* to this original ultimate nature as the immortal being in his perfect (divine) body back from the ordinary creative process of becoming. The most important thing is the stress laid on the body as the medium in which truth can be realised. All the schools of Tantra, hold that the body is the abode of all truth, it is the epitome of the universe. Attempt has been made in Tantra to identify the universe completely with the body. The yogic *sādhanā* is a science of religions: its methodology

→ *haṭha-yoga* or the psychophysical techniques; called *mudrā*, *bandha*, *āsana*, and *prāṇāyāma* (the process of breath-control), and is held that through the proper practice of these processes the flow of semen can be controlled by the *yogin* under all circumstances. In these *mudrās* and *bandhas* the main thing seems to be the acquisition of the capacity for contraction and expansion of some of muscles and nerves associated with the root of penis as well as anus, and with this control of muscles and nerves is often associated the question of breath-control. Among these *mudrās* the most important seems to be the *vajroli*, *sahajoli*, and *amaroli* described in detail in the *Haṭha-yoga-pradīpikā*. As per *Gheraṇḍa Saṁhitā*, 3/45-7, the *khecarī mudrā*, the *mahā-mudrā*, and *yoni-mudrā* are very important. If these *mudrās* and *bandhas* are rightly practised, the flow of semen can be checked at any stage under any condition. The *bandhas* are also the contraction and tightening up, as it were, of many of the muscles and nerves. Among them the *uḍḍiyāna-bandha*, the *jālandhara-bandha*, the *mūla-bandha*, and the *mahā-bandha* are very effective for the purpose. But in this yogic practice of the arrest of the downward flow of semen and of giving it an upward flow to make it reach the *sahasrāra-cakra* of Hindu Tantra and *uṣṇīśa-kamala* of Buddhist Tantra and make it motionless there, the control of different kinds of vital winds is absolutely necessary. There is very close relation between the motion of semen, the vital wind, and the *citta*, and the relation is so intimate that the arrest of anyone of them will stop the course of the other two. It has been said that the *bindu* will attain exactly the same state as the vital wind, and both of them move and stop in perfect correspondance (*amṛta-siddhi*). Nagendra Nath Upadhyaya, *Tāntric Bauddha Sādhanā aur Sāhitya* (in Hindī), pp. 3-15; *Haṭha-yoga-pradīpikā*, tr. Pancham Singh, (III.83-8); T.N. Mishra, *Impact of Tantra on Religion and Art*, p. 96.

consists in its analysis of the body and the discovery of all *tattva*s in the nervous system and in the plexus, and thus making the body a perfect medium for realising the ultimate truth. The Nātha *siddha*s believe that the body is the microcosm of the universe; mountain, sea, moon, sun, and river — all that which the world is composed of are within the human body. It is by *haṭha-yoga* that one is able to have total control over the body and mind, so they believe in *kāya-sādhanā*. In the *kāya-sādhanā*, Śiva and Śakti reside in the body, the former in the *mahāsukha sthāna* (*sahasrāra*) which is the highest cerebral region, and latter in the *mūlādhāra*, the lowest extremity of the spinal cord. Śiva is the noumenal aspect or pure consciousness and perfect rest, and Śakti is the phenomenal aspect of the world activity, the aspect of change and evolution. The *haṭha-yogī* believes that the region below the navel is the region of Śakti, the domain of *pravr̥tti*, activity and change, while the region above the navel is the region of Śiva, the domain of *nivr̥tti*, of rest. And the *sādhanā* consists in rousing the Śakti residing in the region of *pravr̥tti* to unite with the Śiva residing in the region of *nivr̥tti*. The bliss proceeding from the union of Śiva and Śakti is the highest realisation. And this union of Śiva and Śakti symbolises, in the wider sense, the stoppage of the ordinary process of becoming and retrogression of the whole world process for the attainment of the changeless state of Immortal Being. Further, it is said that the right half of the body is Śiva, and the left half, Śakti. Through the nerve *piṅgalā* in the right flows the *apāna vāyu* (wind) which is the stream of Śiva. Likewise, through the nerve *iḍā* flows the *prāṇa-vāyu* (wind) which is the stream of Śakti. The aspirant, through yogic efforts, has to bring these two streams into the middle nerve which is *suṣumnā*. If this is achieved, there will be a perfect equilibrium of Śiva and Śakti, and the yogic union is supposed to be the cause of *mahāsukha* (great bliss), arising, when one experiences absolute non-duality. If one can realise the truth of the body (*bhāṇḍa*), one can also realise the truth of the universe (*brahmāṇḍa*).

According to the views of *yogī*s, there are thirty-two *nāḍī*s (nerve channels) within the body.[4] The energy which has its seat below the

4. S.B. Dasgupta, *An Introduction to Tantric Buddhism*, pp. 153-4.

navel, flows up through three channels. The topmost is called *mahāsukha sthāna* (the place of great bliss. The topmost station is imagined to be a lotus having either sixty-four or thousand petals. Various names are given to the nerve-channels, and among them *lalanā*, *rasanā* and *avadhūti* are the most important, for they combine in themselves, at particular stations, the current supplied by the rest. The *avadhūti* is the middle channel and corresponds to the *suṣumnā* of the Hindu Tantra, while the other two correspond to the *iḍā* and *piṅgalā*. There are also a number of stations, compared to the lotuses (wheel = *cakra*)[5] within the body, and psychic energy in its upward march has to pass through them. The ultimate goal is the creation of the state of *sahaja* which is one of great bliss. It is a state which is without beginning and without end, a state which is free from duality. When this state is attained, the objective world disappears from view, and all the aggregates, elements, and senses merge in it. The *sādhaka* then finds himself to be the sole reality, identical with the universe, and with Śiva (who is ever free).

The purification of and control over the muscles, sinews, nerve, ducts, and nerve centres through the process of *āsana* (posture), *dhauti* (washing), *bandha* (different kind of arrest), *mudrā*, *prāṇāyāma*, and other processes of *haṭha-yoga*[6] are generally prescribed to be directed towards the final aim of transformation and transubstantiation of the body. The question of transubstantiation is the question of attaining full control over the mind. The trend of idealism is also found in the stories of the Nātha literature. And it is true that the control of the mind is the *yoga par-excellence*, and it is held that the vital wind is the vehicle of this mind, and the control of the vital wind through the process of *prāṇāyāma* leads to the control of the mind. With the arrest of the vital wind, the mind becomes arrested, and it is for this reason that the arrest of the vital wind has been held very important in the Nātha literature

---

5. In the *Ṛgveda*, the word *cakra* is used with references to sun (*sūrya*) and the earth, and human body is defined or compared with *cakra*. *Ṛgveda*, I.164.1; *Atharvaveda*, IX.9.1-2, and IX.9.11; *Kaṭhopaniṣad*, I.33.

6. As per *Haṭha-yoga-pradīpikā*, the *haṭha-yoga* really signifies the union of *ha*, i.e., the sun and *ṭha*, the moon.

as well as in the literature of other Yoga schools. It is told by Nātha *siddhas* that through the fire of Yoga (purifying process of Yoga), the ordinary body of changes and decay is burnt away.[7] This school is based on the belief in the two aspects of the Absolute Reality, represented by the sun (*sūrya*) and the moon (*candra*). The sun stands for the principle of destruction (*kālāgni*) through the process of death and decay, and the moon stands for the principle of immutability.

The final aim of Nātha *siddhas* is the attainment of the non-dual state, through the attainment of immortality, in a perfect and divine body. This non-dual state of immortality, which is the state of Maheśvara (Great Lord), can be attained only through the union, rather than the commingling of the sun and the moon.

The main *sāddhanā* of Nātha *siddhas* had to do with the culturing of the body (*kāya-sādhanā*), implying transub-stantiation of the body first into a subtle ethereal body, and then, finally, into an immutable divine body having an eternal existene. The moon, which is the repository of *soma* or *amṛta* (nectar or embrosia) which gives immortality, is situated just below the *sahasrāra*, the lotus of thousand petals in the cerebrum region facing downwards. The quintessence of the visible body is distilled in the form of *soma* in the moon, this *soma* rejuvenates the body and makes it immortal. In the ordinary course, this *soma* trickles down from

7. In the *Siddhānta-paddhati* we find that the physical body emerges from the collection of five factors, viz., *karma* (activity), *kāma* (desire), *candra* (the moon), *sūrya* (the sun), and *agni* (fire). Of these, the first two are rather the conditions of the visible body (*piṇḍa*) while the other three are the primary elements out of which the body is made. Of these three, again, the sun and fire are generally held the same. Then, the primary elements out of which the visible body is made are reduced to two, viz., the sun and the moon. The moon represents the element of *rasa* or *soma* (i.e., the quintessence in the form of juice) and the sun is the element of fire, and therefore, the body is called the product of *agni* and *soma*. *Rasa,* as a *soma*, is the food (*upabhogya*) while fire, as the consumer, is the eater *bhoktā*, (*Gītā*, 15, 13-14), and through the well proportioned combination of the consumer and the consumed, the whole creation is sustained. The sun and the moon as *agni* and *soma* respectively are manifested in the physical world as the seed of the father and the ovum of the mother, through the combination of which proceeds the visible body, and thus *agni* and *soma* are the two primordial elements of which the whole creation is made.

the moon above and is dried up by the sun, the fire of destruction situated in the navel plexus; this drying up of the *soma* by the sun leads an ordinary being to decay and death.[8] This *soma* (also known as *mahārasa*, the great juice) must be protected from the sun.

According to Nāthism, the Ultimate Reality has two aspects which are symbolised by the sun and moon; while the sun is *kālāgni*,[9] the principle of death and destruction, the moon, on the other hand, is the symbol of unchangeability. The aim of a Nātha aspirant is to feel within his own self the ideal of non-duality which is possible by the attainment of immortality and the renovation of the body; Generally Śiva represents this non-dual state, and its attainment is possible by connecting the forces of the sun and moon within the body. The essence which helps the human body to survive is produced from the *soma*, identified also as the moon, which is the source of the drug of immortality (*amṛta*) and which

8. In Yoga texts the moon and sun represent the two elements underlying physical existence, viz., the element of creation and preservation, and the element of change and destruction. The moon as the principle of non-change and immortality resides in the region of Śiva, and the sun as the principle of change and destruction resides in the region of Śakti. Thus, the moon and the sun are associated with Śiva and Śakti. It is said that *bindu* which is the quintessence of the body is of two kinds — the yellowish white *bindu* and red *bindu*, the former is the nature of semen (*śukra*), while the latter is of the nature of ovum (*mahārajas*). The *bindu* (of white colour to suggest the comparison with seed or semen) is contained in the moon in the upper region, while the red *bindu* (*rakta* or red colour to suggest the comparison with ovum) is contained in the sun in the navel (generally the sun is described in the navel, but in the *Gorakṣa Saṁhitā*, chapter IV, verse 152, and *Kaula-jñāna-nirṇaya*, chapter II, verse 3, it is described in the lowest plexus or the *mūlādhāra*); white *bindu* is Śiva and that is the moon, and the latter is Śakti, which is the sun. Therefore, it seems that the conceptions of the moon and the sun have been associated with that of Śiva and Śakti and metaphysically the moon and the sun represent the nature of Śiva and Śakti, respectively.

9. In the *Kaula-jnāna-nirṇaya* (chapter two) this *kālāgni* as Rudra is associated with Śakti, and is said to be seated in the lower region (*mūlādhāra*) within the mouth of Vāḍava. It is held that these seven lower regions are called *pātāla*, and the seven upper regions are called heaven. Creation is sustained as long as the *kālāgni* remains in the lower regions, but when it burns upward dissolution starts.

is found in the *sahasrāra* or the cerebral region of the body. If it is properly utilised, one can attain immortality. But, there is difficulty in that, the *amṛta* dropped from the *soma* or the moon is consumed by the sun which resides in the navel region.[10] However, there is a serpent-like channel within the body having two faces known as *baṅkanāla* or *śaṅkhinī*, and the face from which the *amṛta* is dropped is known as the tenth door (*daśa-dvāra*).[11]

The door can be closed, and this is possible, and it is achieved only by *kāya-sādhanā* (the disciplining of the body). The Hara-Gaurī conception of Nāthism is an adaptation of both the Mahāyānic *karuṇā* and *śūnyatā*, and Vajrayānic *upāya* and *prajñā*. Nāthism believes in three kinds of *śūnya* — *ādi-śūnya*, *madhya-śūnya*, and *antaḥ-śūnya* (the Śūnyavāda of the Mādhyamika system is also accepted in Nāthism). The *śūnya* is to be realised through the Yoga. By the yogic control of breath, the thirty-knots in the spinal cord can be loosened, as a result of which the vital winds, *prāṇa* and *apāna* can enter the spinal cord and move as *haṁsa* through the six nerves plexuses — *mūlādhāra*, *svādhiṣṭhāna*, *maṇipūraka*, *anāhata*, *viśuddha*, and *ājñā*, and on reaching the *sahasrāra* region, assume the nature of *śūnya*. There are 7200 nerves within the body of which sixty-four can be distinctly located and fifteen utilised for yogic purposes.

The human body, which is called *brahmāṇḍa* (the golden egg or the *aurā* of *Brahman*) is the microcosm. There is the nectar rayed — in its proper place, on the top of the spinal column. With its face downward, it rains nectar day and night. The ambrosia from the moon has two subtle parts — one of these nourishes the body like water of the heavenly river

---

10. The theory of the sun and the moon as stated above, the sun is associated with Śakti and the moon with Śiva, therefore, the moon must be saved from the sun. In the grosser aspect, men must save himself from the woman. Charmed and allured by her, man loses vital energy. In Nātha literature women are regarded as the greatest danger in the path of *yoga-sādhanā* and described as the greatest impediment in the march towards immortality. She has been spoken of as the enchantress of the day and consumer of the night.

11. *Śvetāśvatara Upaniṣad*, III.18.

Gaṅgā, descending as a subtle channel on the left side, while the other ray of ambrosia, brilliant as the milk enters the central nerve of the spinal column in order to maintain and recreate the moon in its proper place on top of the central great axis. At the lower region of the great axis of Meru is the sun, located within the body itself. From the inner sun situated at the navel, a subtle channel emanates to the right side of the body and carries the solar fluid upward by the power of its rays. The *haṭha-yoga-pradīpikā* speaks of these two nerves as day and night. The *Sammohana-tantra* says that the left nerve is the moon because of its mild nature, whereas the nerve in the right is called sun because of its fierce nature. The left nerve is said to carry the seed and the right the ovum, the seed is said to be Śiva — it is moon, and the blood is the Śakti; it is the sun. The nerve in the left is *āli* and the right is the *kālī* which represent the vowels and the consonants.

Esoteric teaching of Nāthism declares that if one truly wishes to advance spiritually, one must work consciously to activate the subtle body. Though the basic ingredient and raw energies exist in everyone, they must be focused and channelled consciously. The emotion and mind should be brought to bear on the conscious evocation of an all-powerful subtle body which can then serve as a source of strength, intelligence, and transcendence. This is one of the most important secrets of the Nātha tradition.

5

Buddhist Art

INDIAN art depicts life as interpreted by religion and philosophy. Ancient Indian art, in all periods of development, was closely associated with the rhythm of life including the life of gods and all living beings on earth. The Indian tradition interprets the living world as a manifestation of god. The symbols of art voice the same truth as our philosophy and myths. The purpose of Indian art has been to communicate great truths to mankind through architectural, sculptural, and pictorial reconstructions of the power that maintains stars in their courses. Every Indian religious structure and art form may be regarded as a replica of an unseen celestial religion. This may also be described as theological and traditional; tradition means a kind of healthy discipline conditioned by belief and prescriptions, which embrace the whole of a civilisation in all its modes and trends.

The image or icon, or any such visible symbol of his deity was the medium through which a devotee could transfer his one-souled devotion to his god. The deities are a product of psychic exercises of the most subtle character, and visualised by the worshipper in the course of intense mediation. These psychic exercises are called the *sādhanā*. The act of *sādhanā* has a special bearing on the history and evolution of the icons.

In the Indian religious thought, the omnipresent god, the creator of the universe, is said to reside in everything, and as much of his presence is felt in the loving heart of a devotee as in stocks and stones. To a *sādhaka* who realises the presence of the supreme *Brahman* within himself there is hardly any need of a temple or a divine image of worship. The image of the gods and goddesses are representations meant for those who cannot realise the divine spirit in their hearts. The thoughts of thinkers made manifest and concretised by various means, such as speech, pictorial and sculptural representations, signs, and symbols, that helped in evolving divine images. In its metaphysical essence, the formless undergoes a definite mode of cosmic operation. It arises from certain movement of life-force that animates all matter, and by a process of expansion and growth or of condensation and construction which causes it to crystallise in uncertain shapes. These, as its outer limiting circumscription, show the nature of its formation (*dhyāna-rūpa*). Lines, forms, and colours are not accidental, but are direct manifestations of these inner forces related to the spiritual reality. All these means have been utilised to depict divinity at the level of the common man in order to lift him up gradually to the sublime height of true realisation.

India is a land of many religious faiths, and even within the same faith there have been many sects and sub-sects, often in sharp differences with one another in respect of beliefs and tenets. All the Indian religions are known to have adopted common norms for the expression of their thoughts and beliefs through the art. Religious differences have hardly been able to divert this norm from its logical course. The norms remain the same for all religions irrespective of subjects depicted. The difference lies only in iconographic contents. The *bhakti* (devotion) gave a significant impetus to the construction of images and houses of gods. Emotional attachment with god was considered a road to salvation (*mokṣa*), the easiest one, and a path open to all. Devotion popularised image-worship, as meditation on the Unmanifested Absolute was considered a difficult process. The relation between the caller and the calling spirit is one of identification. It is called the identity of human mind with the ultimate reality. Worship is the acknowledgement of the magnificence of this supreme reality. From the very beginning, attempts have been made to bring god (the Supreme Being) closer to the needs of man.

The origin of image-worship in India can be traced back to very early times, and the cirumstances behind such a development are not exactly known. The image-worship was probably not unknown to the Vedic peoples but the religion of the Vedas knew no idol-worship. The Jaina denied the existence of a Supreme Being, they recognised the practice of worshipping image of their *tīrthaṁkara*s. The history of image-worship in the Buddhist tradition is being traced back from the first century BC, and it is revealed that the liberal *mahāsāṁghika*s and then the Mahāyānists paved the way for devotees to go for the Buddha images for expressing their devotion, probably to satisfy the religious emotions of lay disciples. Buddha is not a proper name, but an attribute of one who was recognised as having attained wisdom (*bodhi*), that cuts the darkness of ignorance and radiates illumination. It is a historical fact that Siddhārtha Gautama, a prince, took the path of an *arhat* at an early stage of his youthful life, and since he belonged to the Śākya clan, came, in due course of time, to be known as Śākyamuni. He was recognised to have reached the highest peak of *bodhi*, and therefore, called Buddha. We do not have any record how Siddhārtha looked before he attained the enlightenment. Buddhist literature has made it clear that the followers of this religion paid homage to their Master (Buddha) through a series of symbols, which were traditionally related to the Buddha, and accepted by the followers to relate and interpret the life and activities of the Master. He was still regarded as an historical person who once lived in flesh and blood. This was probably due to the fact that Master was basically a teacher, and not a saviour god, and those who were orthodox were anxious to avoid any form of worship while hoarding the Buddha relics in reverence. But the convention was shortly to disappear. The figure of *bodhisattva* (who requires certain parameters to qualify himself for the attainment of Buddhahood) was the first to be introduced. But this covention too was shortly to disappear. Many social and religious, and ethnic and cultural forces lay at the back of this basic transformation of a monastic religion directed towards individual salvation to a religion and a way of life oriented towards the salvation of all sentient beings. In this process, the mortal historical Buddha, was transformed into an idealised abstraction, but he came to be defied. The *bhakti* (devotion) or that cult of *bhakti*[1] denotes primarily the loving adoration of some persons by others; but secondarily, the deeply affectionate and mystic devotion for some personal deity who is the object of worship. There was the belief on one person (Buddha) as the spiritual being, the faith that his power is sufficient to secure, and the goodwill prevailed, and the conception of the nexus binds together *tathāgata* and worshippers. That *bhakti* and the ritual of worship, were already prevailing (current) during the period in the shape and form of the worship and prayer to the relics (*stūpa*), and symbols must have contributed to this transformation. There were also other force at work that had entered the folds of the faith and many of them came from that tradition where worship of images of gods and goddesses were prevalent. These factors must have contributed to the deification of the Buddha. Once divinity was attributed to him, iconographic types of Buddha made their appearance in art with the Indian conception of a great man (*mahāpuruṣa lakṣaṇa*s).

Under the impact of the Mahāyāna philosophy, the image of the Buddha made its appearance. It seems that, the Buddha was no longer a human teacher (preacher of wisdom) but an eternal principle that had made itself manifest in human form for the salvation of mankind, as an embodiment of universal love and infinite compassion. Buddha's last words were that decay is inherent in all component beings. Workout your own salvation with diligence. At this stage of evolution of the idea of the Buddha, to exhibit on the conceptual level, a melting quality was evolved in the expression of his face and in the texture of his body. This feature was conceived, and as in his supreme wisdom (*prajñā*), he had realised that the world was full of sufferings and miseries, his likeness was realised as if his mind and heart were always melting in love and compassion.

---

1. *Śvetāśvatara Upaniṣad*, VI.23.

In Hīnayāna (early Buddhism), particularly in its earlier phase no worship was offered to any image by any Buddhist. Buddha did not believe in gods or worship. In Buddhist art also, Buddha images were not met in the schools of early narrative of art such as Sāñcī, Bodh Gayā, and Bhārhūt. But the symbols related to Buddha were freely represented to indicate the presence of the Buddha.[2] In other words, the earlier phases of Buddhism are more or less free from the iconic representations of gods and goddesses. Only scenes from Buddha's life, and *Jātaka* stories were given preference in the earlier Buddhism. Buddha was deified in Mahāyāna which considered him to be *lokottara* (supra-human), and attributed to him even divine powers and qualities. According to Mahāyānists, the Buddha was glorified as an eternal universal principle comparable to *śūnyatā* or *tathatā* or *dharma-dhātu*. Therefore, this transcendental Buddha was described as of without origin and decay, without name and without form. How could then they explain the physical reality of the historical Siddhārtha? Therefore, this led to the introduction of a new concept of Buddhism that had its reflection on the iconography. That new concept was the theory of *trikāya* or the three bodies of Buddha. This three-fold division was of a philosophical nature and was designated as *dharma-kāya* (word of Buddha) which was the real one, that was eternal, infinite, and without birth death and form; *saṁbhoga-kāya* (body of bliss), the form which the Buddha at times assumed for the satisfaction of *bodhisattva*s and his advanced devotees, a richly adorned and brightly effluent form with *mahāpuruṣa lakṣaṇa*s made manifest, and *nirmāṇa-kāya* or *rūpa-kāya* (nominal body), the

---

2. The *stūpa*s received worship even in the life-time of the Buddha, and this continued throughout the centuries. The *stūpa*, as an image of the Buddha, containing relics, which was honoured as the symbol of the departed, had disappeared. So *stūpa* became a necessary cult object in every Buddhist monastic establishment. It is the idea of the Buddha that is worshipped. This is the *dharma-kāya*, the body of very Buddha itself, which is the symbol of a departed manifestation of Buddha. Therefore, the *stūpa* can be identified with the Buddha's holy persons, but at the same time it stands for the event of his entry into *nirvāṇa*, by implication, the final goal of enlightenment in the general Buddhist sense. Thus, *stūpa* became a monument embodying the absolute truth and symbol of his perennial abode.

material or created body, an earthly form which is the historical Buddha assumed for the guidance and satisfaction of common beings. The historical or mortal Buddha, according to Mahāyānists, was the embodiment of *rūpa-kāya* or *nirmāṇa-kāya* of the real, formless Buddha. So, it is clear that there could be an image of the Buddha in terms of the last two *kāyas* alone, and one may perhaps speculate that the Buddha image of the Mahāyānists conception were visual articulation of the *saṁbhoga-kāya* of the Buddha, since all Buddha images in general can be said to represent his *rūpa-kāya*, including those that can be explained in Hīnayānist terms also. A further development was the creation of mystical Buddhas for the four directions and one for the centre of the world; the group of Buddhas of this theory is called the five *dhyānī* Buddhas. It is in the *guhya-samāja* that the idea of a pantheon, rationally classified and systematically crystallised has been enumerated. These *dhyānī* Buddhas represent the five cosmic elements of which the world is composed of. They are described as the progenitors of the five *kulas* or the families of gods and goddesses. It is in this way that the Buddhists built a well classified pantheon with its multiplicity of gods and goddesses, and when these were represented in art, they were required to show their origin by holding on their heads the miniature figure of their parental *dhyānī* Buddha. These five *dhyānī* Buddhas are endowed with five different body colours in their *sādhanās*. White is prescribed for Vairocana, it symbolises delusion; Ratnasambhava is yellow, that denotes pride; Akṣobhya is blue bodied, which stands for hatred; Amitābha's red body signifies passion; and the green colour of Amoghasiddhi symbolises envy.[3] The artists had a considerable hand in executing the images, and they introduced their own traditions and innovations. In its purview, Vajrayāna included all varieties of attractive tenets, notions, dogmas, theories, rites, and practices, and incorporated all that best in other religions. It satisfied everybody and all ranks of the people and devotees. Its popularity became an established fact. One of the chief topics dealt with in Vajrayāna is the deity. Vajrayāna brought

---

3. *Guhyasamāja-tantra*, ed. B. Bhattacharya, chapter 13.

advaya or non-duality in the conception of the Yab-Yum form of deities in which the deity appears locked in close embrace with his Śakti or the female counterpart. The last phase of the religious salvation was offered through Tāntric worship, which essentially meant devotion paid to the female energy or Śakti, which in its grosser aspects encouraged sexual practices as a means of salvation. Such scenes are found represented in stone, metal, and paper (painting). The votaries also accordingly as they wanted to have their gods in a powerful form, added extra hands, heads, and feet to suit their own ideas, and it is precisely in this way that the deities increased to a large number. The imagination on the part of the sculptors and also the product of their chisels were very greatly influenced by the spirit of the age in which they flourished, as well as by the situation in which they worked. The Tāntric rites in which the images were used had certain influences. The excavations and explorations have brought to light a large number of images of Buddhist gods and goddesses belonging to the Tāntric School.

The art of sculpture and painting attained a state of perfection in ancient India that could stand comparison with what was attained in other countries. The Indian artist was not wanting in originality and vigour in the handling of his subjects. He tried to remain true to the nature, and in the representation of birds and animals, he remained often unsurpassed. Throughout the ages, Indian art evinces a consistent growth, each succeeding phase starting with the heritage of the preceding one and leading the style to their natural and logical fulfilment. Religious urge has been behind the full efflorescence of art styles. In early periods of the history of Indian art, the imagination of the artist was not tied down by any religious prescription which, however, became the bane of art in later times. One of the characteristic features of Indian art and architecture is the quality it derives by using motifs rich in symbolism and mythical imagery. An early factor that brought about visible changes in the natural and progressive state of Indian art was the introduction of Tantric ideas in worship of Hindus as well as Buddhists.

In the following lines, an attempt is being made to study the influence of Buddhism and the impact of Tantrism in Buddhist art. To begin with the reference that every incident of Buddha's life, real or legendary mentioned in texts was recorded in terms of the Buddhist art. Every incident of Buddha's life, was recorded in terms of sculpture and painting, and every spot associated with Lord Buddha's life turned into a centre of Buddhist pilgrimage by his followers where they erected structures in the memory of the Master. In Buddhist monuments faithful recording of Buddha's life and activities were done. Monasteries, provided shelter to Buddha and his homeless disciples during the raining season, and these already came into existence during the life-time of the Master. Being wandering (*parivrājaka*) monks, the member of the *saṁgha* had at first no fixed habitat. They stayed here and there in a forest, on a hill side, in a mountain cave, and in open air;[4] they were compelled to find out some temporary shelter, whether in caves or under trees or sanctuaries, during the three months of the rainy season. To avoid rain (*varṣā*) they opted for a fixed abode (*āvāsa*), and they depended largely on alms from the house holders around the *āvāsa*. This state of affairs took a better turn even during the life-time of Buddha. On one occasion, Buddha not being an advocate of extreme asceticism, accepted the offer of dwelling places at Rājagṛha offered by a local merchant for the use of *saṁgha*. Thus came into being monastic abodes where the *bhikṣus* could meditate at place, and in these retreats they performed the communal ceremonies. These monasteries were built up by Buddha's lay devotees and admirers, who thus set a custom which was subsequently taken up by royal personages. It is significant that the merchant class was one of the main supporters of the growing Buddhist order and Buddhist monastic settlements which had first been founded close to towns and villages, and whose interested support was necessary for the material requirements for the monks, now began to grow up close to important trade routes, where simple lodging might be available for the travellers, and where gifts might be expected in return.

Before departing from the earth Buddha himself had suggested to his disciple *ānanda* about his last will. 'How should we honour the body

---

4. *Cullavagga*, tr. I.B. Horner, *Sacred Book of the Buddhist,* XX, p. 204.

or relic bones of the *tathāgata*' asked Ānanda to the Master, and Buddha replied that 'in the same manner they raise the *stūpa* on the crossing of four high way on the relics of a *cakravartī* king'. He further suggested that 'you should also erect a *stūpa* for *tathāgata*'. According to this injunction a *stūpa* was an emblem of a *cakravartī* king and a great man.[5] Buddha was also *cakravartī* king before becoming a great being (*mahāyogī* or Buddha). And he won over other sects of religion of that time owing to his religious preaching. So, he became a *dharma-jayī* (conqueror of religion). The symbolism of *stūpa*, thereby, was associated with the nature of Buddha as *cakravartī* and Buddha as a *mahāyogī*. It was truly an object of worship symbol of Buddha's great demise. *Stūpa*s, symbolising iconically the Master, remained popular for a long time, and became nearly the sole object of worship among the Buddhists in the absence of his icon.

Aśoka, the great Maurya Emperor took leading role in the extension of Buddhism. Being impressed by the message of Śākyamuni, he employed all his resources for dissemination of the religion. The new life which Aśoka infused into the religion of Śākyamuni and the impetus which he gave to the Buddhist building arts were not extinguished when the Maurya empire fell into pieces. The tradition continued during the periods of the Kaṇvas (first century BC) in north and Sātavāhans and Ikṣvākus (first century BC to third century AD) in the Deccan and south-eastern India. During the regime of these powerful dynasties, the building activities continued on an accelerated pace. The wealth specially of the rich mercantile community, was utilised in erecting Buddhist edifices. Every Buddhist tried to contribute whatever he could, the poor came forward with their offer of skill and labour which led to the introduction of large number of Buddhist monuments and *caitya*s. The period also

---

5. The Buddhists were not the first to raise *stūpas*, far less the innovations of that. Their architecture and art in their practical application are virtually indistinguishable from Indian architecture and art in general. Throughout all ages, Buddhist architecture and sculptures, have shared the main trends of Indian art in technique, style, and form, the iconographical concepts being the main criterion in differentiating religious diffusions.

witnessed the growth and development of Buddhist rock-cut architecture. The idea of rock-cut caves was derived from natural caves. The cave was therefore, not an innovation of Buddhists. It was in a way even earlier. Out of the live rock, the Buddhist made beautiful monasteries (*vihāras*) for congregated monastic life and *caitya-gṛha*. The Indian art was still essentially descriptive and narrative in form and content, that was the time when artists told stories, through reliefs, of the Master in a simple manner. The monuments at Dhaulī, Bhāja, Karlā, Bedas, Piṭhalkhora, Kānherī, and Nāsik are all, in some way or the other affiliated to the Buddhist way of life. The half finished forepart of an elephant at Dhaulī included in the context of the birth of the Buddha, and the elephant was certainly regarded as a very important symbol of the Buddhist religion.

The beginning of the Christian era was an important landmark in Buddhist religion and art when under the impact of Mahāyāna ideology, the images of the Buddha made their way, a literary articulation of which, one finds in Aśvaghoṣa's *Buddhacarita*. The king Kaniṣka, the great ruler of Kuṣāna dynasty is particularly remembered for his patronage in the Buddhist religion and art; during his regime the fourth Buddhist council was convened to discuss various interpretations of Buddha's saying as given by different teachers. This council marked a fundamental division in the *saṁgha* and Buddhist doctrines. The goal of this new form of Buddhism was the salvation of all beings, as distinct from the notion of salvation of the Hīnayānist. By introducing certain new ideas in the religion, the Mahāyānist secured the support of the masses. Buddha was no longer considered a teacher whose presence was to be indicated by symbols; he was deified, and the common mind was satisfied by embellishing and worshipping ceremonially the images of saviour with prayers and incantations of the god redeeming grace. From the Master, Buddha became a Lord. The introduction of the image of Buddha met with universal approval. His icon was conceived on the Indian notion of a great man (*mahā-puruṣa*) with his distinctive marks (*lakṣaṇas*), and thereby introduced the image of the Master. It is believed that in the Gāndhāra region, the first image of the Lord was carved out in stone. But the scholars are divided in their opinion regarding the place as to where the first image of the Buddha was carved: A number of sculptures, delineating in great detail the incident of Buddha's life from birth to death, real and legendary, as gathered from Buddhist texts and tradition were also produced.

The original Hīnayānist conception of the Buddha was that the Master was an omniscient human being of superior wisdom, but at later stage they attributed in him super-human powers and qualities. The Gāndhāra Buddha of early centuries of Christian era, or the *bodhisattva* figure of Mathurā (second or third century AD), can be explained in Hīnayānist terms. These images represented the Buddha as seated in meditation or in *abhaya-mudrā*, relating him, thereby, to the Hīnayānist interpretation of *dhyāna-yoga* as given in *Dīgha Nikāya*.[6] The Buddhist concept of the technique *dhyāna-yoga* hardly differed from the knowledge and practice of other contemporary Indian religions. The Mahāyānist had, however, a different conception of the Buddha who according to them was an eternal universal principal. The Yogācāra school of Buddhist thought of Asaṅga and Vasubandhu seems to have been a direct response to this movement. The image of Sārnāth achieves all this and even more in the number of seated or standing images of the Buddha or *bodhisattva* that have come down to us. It was at Sārnātha that the Buddha preached his first sermon, and this event is referred to in Buddhist texts as the Turning of the Wheel of Law (*dharma-cakra-pravarttana*). The event was represented by the figure of a seated Buddha with two hands held in front of the chest in *dharma-cakra-pravarttana-mudrā*. When one stands before this image and observes it for a while with an intent gauge, one finds that the Lord is illumined from within himself, withdrawn altogether from the visible world, and enjoying the beatitude of ineffable bliss from within which is the ideal state of a *yogī*. Here is indeed the fulfilment in concrete visual terms of the evolved idea of *bodhi* and its embodiment in the image. But, the emergence of Buddha image did not effect the excavation of rock-cut *caitya-gṛha*. On the contrary, it was practised on a greater scale at places like Ajantā, Ellorā, and Bāgh where

6. *Dīgha Nikāya*, *sūtra* No. 22.

images were carved and cave walls were decorated with paintings. During this period Buddhism received and experienced an unparalleled intellectual and philosophical vision of the Vaibhāṣikas and Sautrāntikas on the one hand and Mādhyamikas and Yogācārins on the other. Indeed, the Buddhism had come to enjoy a most enviable position in India's socio-religious life; the idealistic Vijñānavāda had in fact touched a point in wisdom after which there was hardly anything left for further exploration. These were the outcomes of centuries growth and efflorescence what has been called Buddhist art, the peak point of which was attained in the fifth and sixth centuries at Sārnāth, Mathurā, Ajantā, and Ellorā, for instance. There was hardly anything left for further exploration in Buddhist art.

All important religious sects of the country — Hindu, Jaina, and Buddhist presented sensuous and erotic motifs in their art. Sensuous representation in art was a pan-Indian cultural feature. It implies a common cultural substratum which influenced religious sects all over India. This common substratum is seen in those beliefs and practices which show the primal connection between sex and religion. Far from being suppressed, sex played an important part in the religious life of early communities and civilisations. It was realised that it was necessary to experiment in art before conventionalising the aspect in texts. Forms, once accepted in art, have a tendency to become conventionalised and assume the character of motifs. In the culture of India which glorifies traditional values, the process of conventionalisation became a major factor leading to persistence and inertia in the use of motifs. The religious structures were the means to express the above-mentioned philosophy and motifs. The secular subjects drawn from everyday life were introduced in the *stūpa* architecture also. The religious theme gradually received an artistic treatment, with the result that it turned into an art motif. The process of secularisation and sensualisation is clearly noticeable in *stūpa* architecture, various reliefs adorning *stūpa*s at Amarāvatī and Nāgārjunakoṇḍa. But, the Āndhra School emphasises depiction of scenes in the life of the Buddha prior to the enlightenment, specially his life before abandoning *saṁsāra*, his stay in harem, the luxuries of the court, etc. The depiction is more sensuous than religious. The art was hardly religious at all, and far less Buddhist; it does not speak of nor aim at suggesting the Buddhist ideal of renunciation or *nirvāṇa* or discipline or strict ethical virtues including avoidance of woman. Rather, it is frankly naturalistic and essentially sensuous. The disciplined body and conquered mind happen to have been the characteristics of the art of the Gupta period. The relief sculptures of Amarāvatī and particularly of Nāgārjunakoṇḍa revealed the fact that all dramatist personnel are seemingly engaged in enjoying their life for the last time before entering into a stage of detachment and discipline which are the key notes of the classical art of the Gupta period. The treatment rendered in art is, no doubt, artistic and poetic. But we must remember that these motifs are all placed just next to Buddhist scenes. There must have been something in the social climate of the time that encouraged the use of erotic motifs as a form of embellishment in religious art.

In the art expression at Ajantā, one finds a complete statement of indivisible union of sacred and secular art. In the Ajantā wall paintings one feels a definite departure from the art of early Buddhism where emphasis was more on symbolic expressions keeping, thereby, away from the world of reality. Ajantā paintings offered a sort of religious romanticism imbued with lyric quality, a reflection encompassing every aspect of life as such in the spiritual sense, and as an aspect of the divine. Sensuous physical beauty became an emblem of spiritual beauty. Hence, it reminded that life has become an art, but the ultimate goal of it was never forgotten.

Tantrism was a powerful religious movement which emerged out of the coalescence between primitive magic and highly evolved spiritual ideals. Tāntric practices are older than the written scripture on the subject. Their systematic introduction into Hinduism, Jainism, and Buddhism took place in or about the fifth century AD. The period of seventh to twelfth centuries were the peak period of Tāntric cults of the Hindus, Jainas, and Buddhists. Buddhist Tantrism was prevalent in Orissa, Bengal, and Bihar. The monasteries of Nālandā, Pahārpur, and Ratnagiri particularly and a few other centres in the east in general were centres of Buddhist Tantrism. Images of the time of the Pāla dynasty show Tāntric influences.[7] In the medieval period religious cults influenced by Tantrism accomodated a female partner known as Śakti or *prajñā* with male god. Tāntric literature and beliefs gave momentum to the worship of gods with their consorts which resulted in their introduction in medieval iconography.

In its flourishing days Tāntric form of Buddhism was very strong and active in eastern India, or it can be said that eastern India became the most vital centre of Tāntric Buddhism. Many important Buddhist establishments were founded during the Pāla period. Every monastic establishment, including the Nālandā *mahāvihāra* which existed even before the time of Pālas, came to be active centres of Tāntric Buddhism. The famous *ācārya* (teacher) came forward to advocate the cause of Tāntricism. Chairs for the study and teaching of Tantra were founded in different centres of learning such as Nālandā, Vikramśilā, and Odantapura. They are known to have systematised and perfected this complex and esoteric form of Buddhism, along with rituals. Eminent scholars like Śāntarakṣita worked as Professor of Tantra in the famous university of Nālandā. In fact, the Tantra is a science dealing with psychic

---

7. Buddhism of the Pāla and Sena periods represent that outgrowth of Mahāyāna which is described as Tāntricism, an assimilation of elements of Hindu religion into Buddhism, such as concept of Śakti or female energy of *bodhisattva*, and reliance on magic spells and rituals. The worship of mystical *dhyānī* Buddhas and the crteator, Ādi-Buddha, a Buddhist Brahmā, completely replaced any devotion to the person of the melted Buddha. This phase of Buddhism is described as the Vajrayāna, that together with it popularised of its art, in eighth and ninth centuries. On the principle of Tāntric Śaivism and Vaiṣṇavism, these new interpretations suited the prevailing environment, and hardly disturbed the form and structure of art in any degree. No doubt, Tāntricism contributed to the evolution of multiplicity of iconographic types of form, but they all summarised within the form and structure of contemporary norms. India presents the scene of a cultural milieu in which all divergent elements have been brought together to form a common pattern, the prevailing art stages have mediated among the above sects and denominations in order to bring them all over with existing norms for the purpose of artistic expression of their ideas and thoughts.

matters and give directions for a variety of psychic exercises. Like all other sciences the Tantra is not open to all, but only to those who are initiated into the mysteries of the science, and are competent to follow the prescribed practices. One of the most fundamental point of Tāntric art is that its geometric forms seem to aspire chiefly towards absolute geometrical purity. This purity is not an end in itself, but a symbol or revealed image on an aspect of cosmic structure, in the same way that the very special *mantra* (monosyllabic mystic sound formula) functions. The symbol of form or sound is meant to be used in mental concentration in order to approach the two elements of creation, which are believed to form a polarity such as male and female. When both elements are in complete union, it is an equilibrium to be found, and thus the highest state of bliss is reached. This union of balance is animated by the desire to become manifest, the centre of eternal bliss evolves in form and sound in creation. The theory of mystic diagrams (*yantra*) or mystic circle (*maṇḍala*) aided the *sādhaka* to reach spiritual goal. Such art is not decorative as it is cultic. The true Tāntric art is functionally related to *upāsanā* and *sādhanā* to attain the non-dual *sahaja* state. Lines, forms, and colours are not accidental, but are direct manifestations of the inner forces related to the spiritual reality. With the gradual development of Tāntric Buddhism, the art of painting *yantra* and *maṇḍala*s developed to an enormous extent. Their iconographic richness and cosmic multiplicity made them nothing less than veritable psychocosmograms. Initiation into a specific *maṇḍala* by a teacher (*guru*) became the most effective means of spiritual enlightenment, in which the Tāntric adept tried to identify himself with the origin beyond time and space. Therefore, the Tantra required competent preceptors and efficient disciples. The excavations and explorations have brought to light a large number of images of Buddhist gods and goddesses belonging to the Tantra school. It is needless to say that the Buddhist images discovered in Bihar, Bengal, and Orissa are mostly the product of the Tāntirc School of Buddhism.

In the territory comprised of Bengal, Bihar, and parts of Orissa the Pāla rulers dominated the political and cultural affairs for approximately four centuries, from middle of the eighth to the middle of the twelfth.

The rulers were ardent Buddhist and they patronised the Tāntric form of the religion that had been showing great vitality at that time. Under the Pālas, a school of art of great activity and significance flourished; this school consisted of a plastic style in stone and metal, as well as a pictorial style recognised in contemporary manuscript paintings. A large number of palm-leaf manuscripts of Buddhist texts and a few of their contemporaries, bear painting on the leaves and occasionally on the wooden covers. These manuscript paintings give evidence of the existence of an active and vigorous school of painting in eastern India; a few of these are known to have been produced in famous monasteries like Nālandā, Vikramaśilā, Vikramapura, etc. The impact of this school may be felt in Nepal and Tibet also. For this pictorial style, the appellation Tāntric art may have a greater validity since extant documents are Buddhist, and representations therein are seen to have been inspired by the ideas enunciated in the Tantra. This school advocated the principle of Tāntric ideas of Buddhist thought. This school had its foundation on earlier school, and the form and structure of the school had been clearly defined and established before the Pālas emerged in the political and cultural arena of eastern India, as well as before the active and dominant phase of Tantrism in Buddhist creed. Moreover, the school served other creeds also, and the style remained uniform. There is harldy any deviation, with regard to style, between Brāhmaṇical sculpture and a Buddhist. The school had important links and affiliations with other contemporary schools in northern India. But gradually, the eastern schools of art underwent a change accommodating the expression of Tāntric idea in Buddhism.

Feudal social conditions were the right soil for the development of Tāntric religions. Short-cut devices to *mokṣa*, in contrast to rigorous path of asceticism, were advocated, and their virtues extolled. The feudal atmosphere fastened interest in superstitions and supernatural beliefs. Belief in the magical power of sex reinforced in this atmosphere. In Tāntricism, the practice of *maithuna* was considered as one of the *makāra*s which were offered to the deity for gaining *siddhi*. *Maithuna* and other *makāra*s were believed to have the possibilities to please deities. Tantrism soon became a movement influencing all major religions. It is mainly the rapid spread of Tāntric elements and crystallisation of feudal tendencies that provided a suitable soil for this outburst. They accepted sex for the religious function, but were not supposed to have sexual practices the public. This suggests that it was not meant for the enunciation of Tāntric doctrine or philosophy. It appears that the serious intent of Tāntric practices was lost, and religious practices were reduced to pleasurable activities. With the adoption of a pantheon of gods and goddesses, Buddhism lost its individuality and justification for existence as a separate religion as distinct from Hinduism. The rational and highly ethical teachings of the Buddha were, thus, smoothered under the load of gross superstitions, ritualistic worship of host of deities, and immortal life,[8] against each of which Buddha had led a ceaseless crusade.

What actually happened, however, was that neither a suitable teacher (*guru*) was available nor an adept underwent through the preliminary course of training. Such non-observations of the conditions prescribed in Tantra, inevitably led to abuses. One may thus conclude by saying that no religion or a sect thereof have promulgators of such abuses as did the early Vajrayāna Buddhists.

A manuscript of the *Aṣṭasāhasrikā-prajñāpāramitā* give an information that Tāntric form of Buddhism had left impression on religious art, and describe the subject depicted as per Buddhist texts, and the divinities belong to that religion. During the period when Tāntric ideas dominated Buddhist thought, all Buddhist divinities, irrespective of their affiliations, were required to be worshipped according to Tāntric rituals of *mantra*, *mudrā*, and *maṇḍala*, etc.

For the colours of *maṇḍala*, *Mahāvairocana-sūtra* states that *maṇḍala* should be painted in five colours, viz., interior of the *maṇḍala* in white colour followed by red, yellow, blue and black. In *Cakrasaṁbhara-tantra*, it is prescribed that the walls of a *maṇḍala* should be painted in five colours and should maintain the order. In certain *maṇḍala*s, the four directions within the palace are indicated by colours.

8. *Indian Antiquary*, X, p. 344.

The reference to the has also been made in an altogether different context. In the *Kālacakra-tantra*, the four elements — air, fire, water, and earth are identified with four different colours, viz., white and yellow, red, blue, or black respectively.[9] In Tāntric Buddhism, references to five colours are frequently met. These colours were symbolic — black symbolises killing and anger, white denotes rest and thinking, yellow stands for restraining and nourishing, red is for subjugation and summing, and green stands for exorcism.[10] The *Yoga-tantra* symbolises tree *kāya* (body), *vāc* (speech), and *citta* (mind) in three different colours, viz., white, red, and blue. Akṣobhya, who rules *citta-maṇḍala* or *citta-cakra* is represented by blue *vajra*; Amitābha, who presides over *vāc-maṇḍala* or *vāc-cakra* is symbolised as red lotus flowers or red *vajra*, while Vairocana who presides over *kāya* is represented either by a white *vajra* or by a white wheel circle.[11]

The notion of the polarity of colours is found to have been entertained in Tāntric Buddhism. For example, colour black denotes darkness. It is inauspicious, it symbolises *avidyā*, and represents evil. The colour white represents light; it is auspicious, it denotes *vidyā*, and stands for the good. It symbolises delusion, pacification, purity, the element of water, the aggregate of form perceptions, and goodness; the east is indicated by white, maleness, and wisdom of discrimination. White also stands for compassion and perfection of *nirvāṇa*. The red symbolises passion, hatred, subjugation, empowerment, the west, the element of fire, and the aggregate of sensations and preceptions. It symbolises a female and compassion (*karuṇā*) also. Red is the colour of *vajravārāhī* as a sign of her devotion to the service of all sentient beings. The thought of enlightenment (*bodhicitta*) represents the union of *prajñā* (insight) and *upāya* (means) of red and white colours respectively, and this union leads to a great bliss (*mahā-sukha*). Red and white drops flow in the channels of all human beings dissolving into indestructible drops, white at the

9. *Kālacakra-tantra: Exposition of Dalai Lama*, XIV, ed. Jeffery Hopkins.
10. George Christopher, *The Candamaharosana Tantra*, p. 25.
11. *Niṣpannayogāvali*, ed. B. Bhattacharya, pp. 12-13 and *Sādhanamālā*, ed. B. Bhattacharya, p. 218.

top and red at the bottom. Thus, sun is conceived as red and moon as white. In the structural patterns of a *maṇḍala*, the union of *prajñā* (insight) and *upāya* (means) is expressed through male and female deities embracing each other (*yab-yum*), and in this process the discrimination of the two is removed. The white *vajradhara* and black *vajrātmā* dissolve into one.

The colour yellow symbolises pirde, prosperity, affluence, the south, the element of earth, the aggregate of sensations, the wisdom of equality, etc. The colour green denotes envy, the multitude, the element of air, the north, the concept of consciousness, and the accomplishment of wisdom. Green is the combination of white (pacifying), yellow (affluence), and blue (destruction). The goddess Tārā who covers a whole range of such functions is depicted as green. The colour blue symbolises hatred, destruction, killing, the element of space or air, unchangeability, firmness of mind, the wisdom of *dharma-dhātu*, and the aggregate of consciousness.[12]

Besides the five common colours, in Vajrayāna, the colour gold is found to be given adequate importance. The colour gold is mentioned in relation to the time of birth of Gautama, the period of his attainment of enlightenment, and also his demise.

---

12. According to *Kālacakra-tantra*, colour scheme to indicate different directions — the black indicates east, yellow west, white north, and red stands for south.

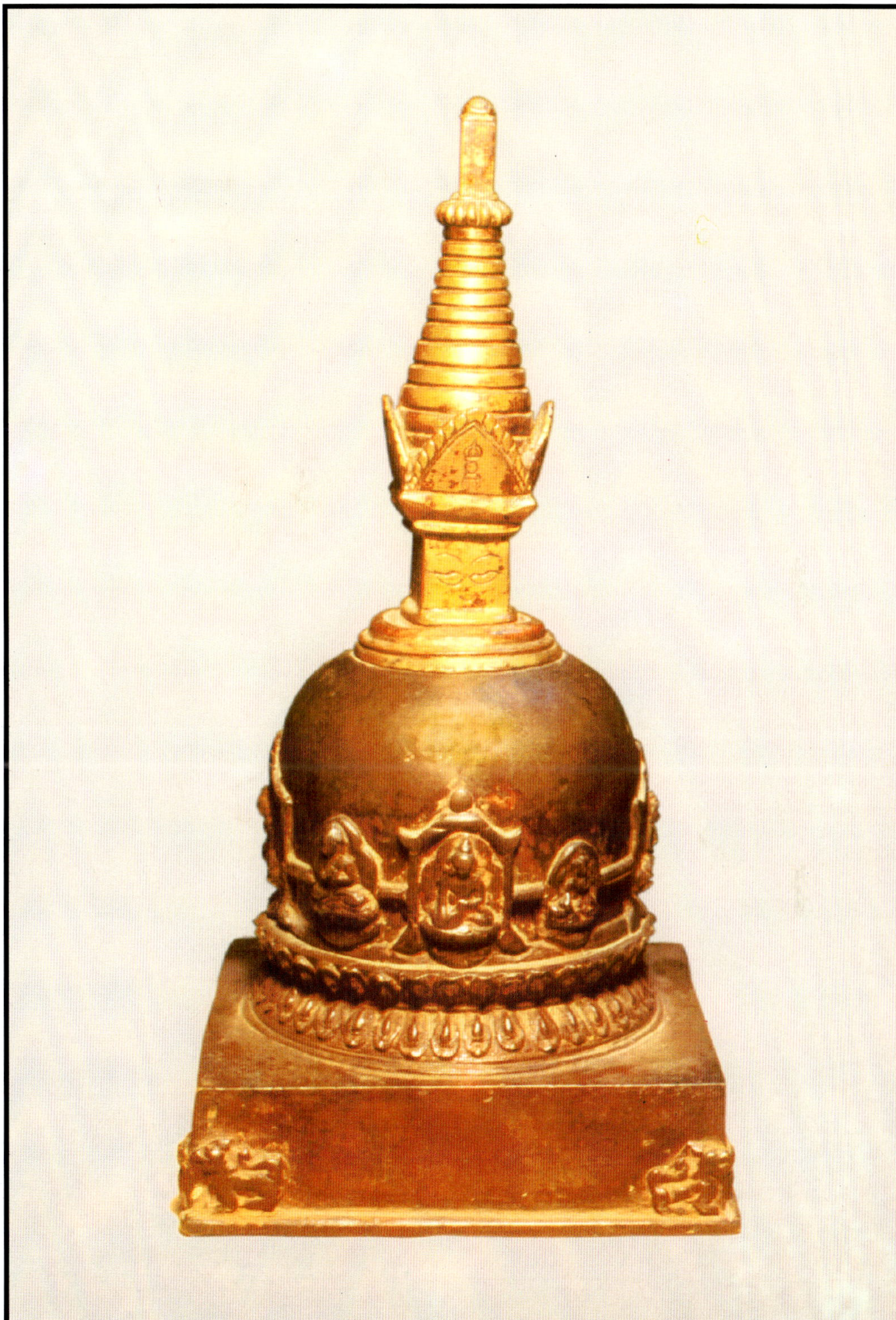

Fig 1: Stūpa

Fig 2: Ugratārā Yantra

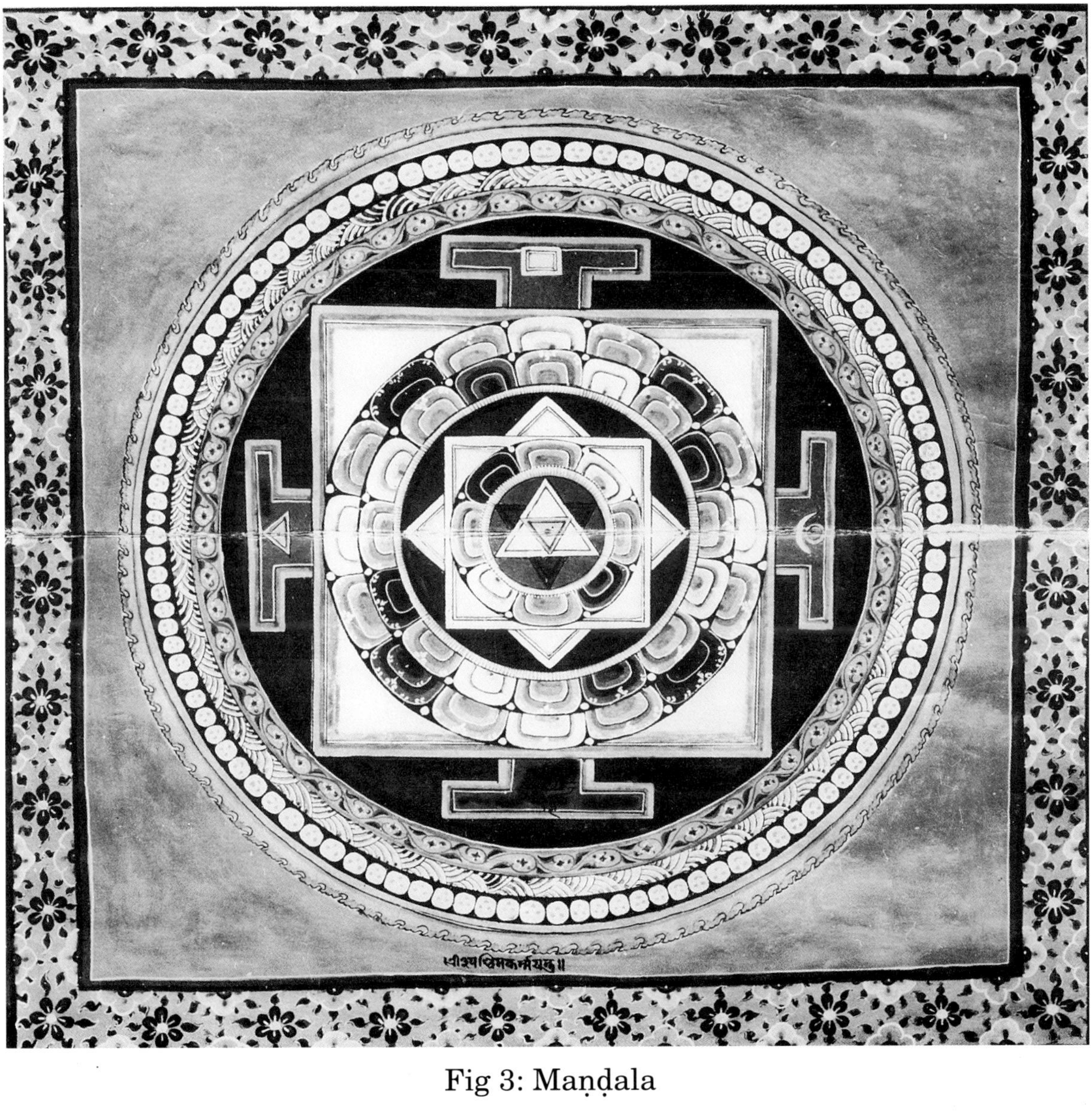

Fig 3: Maṇḍala

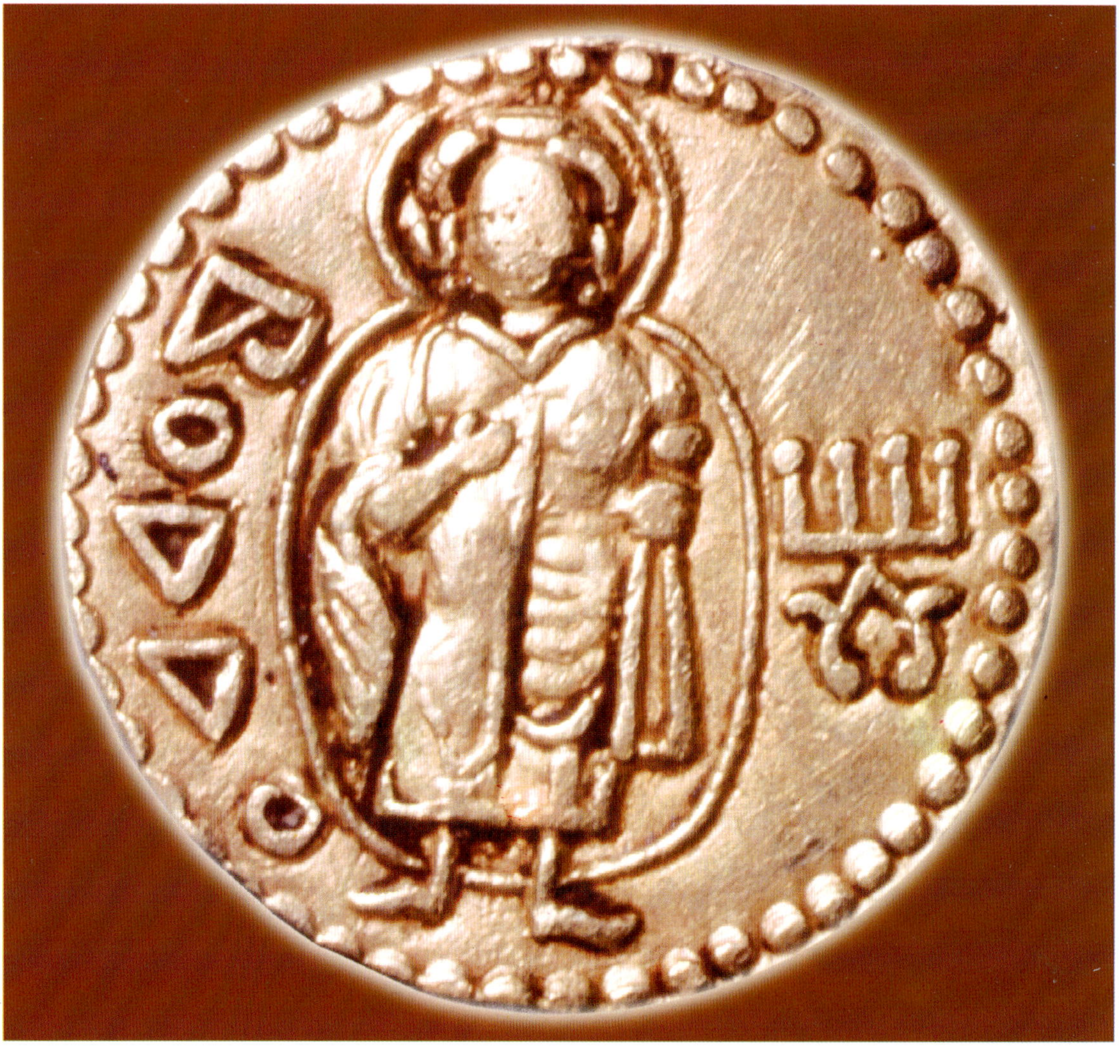

Fig 4: Buddha (gold coin)

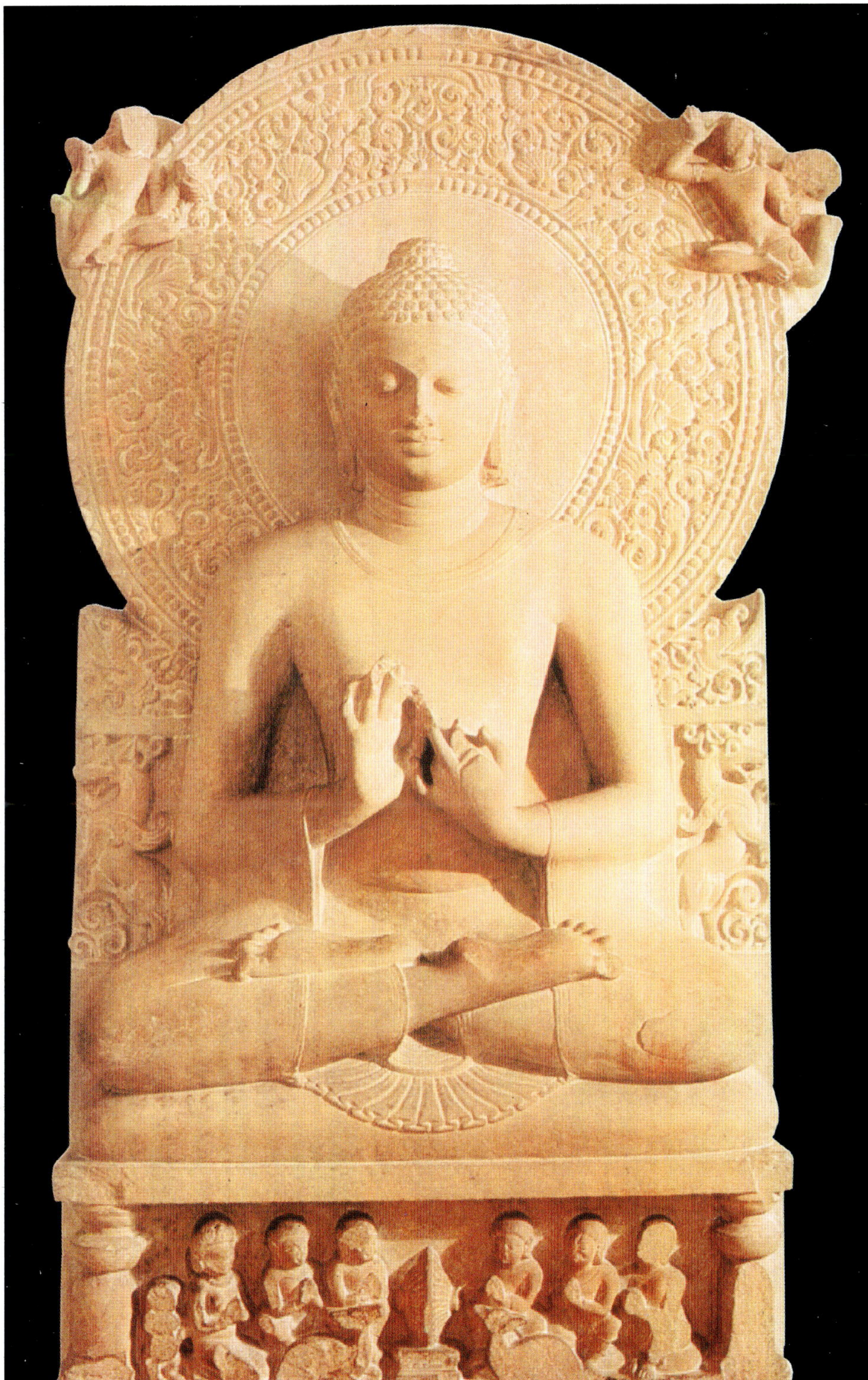

Fig 5: Buddha (stone)

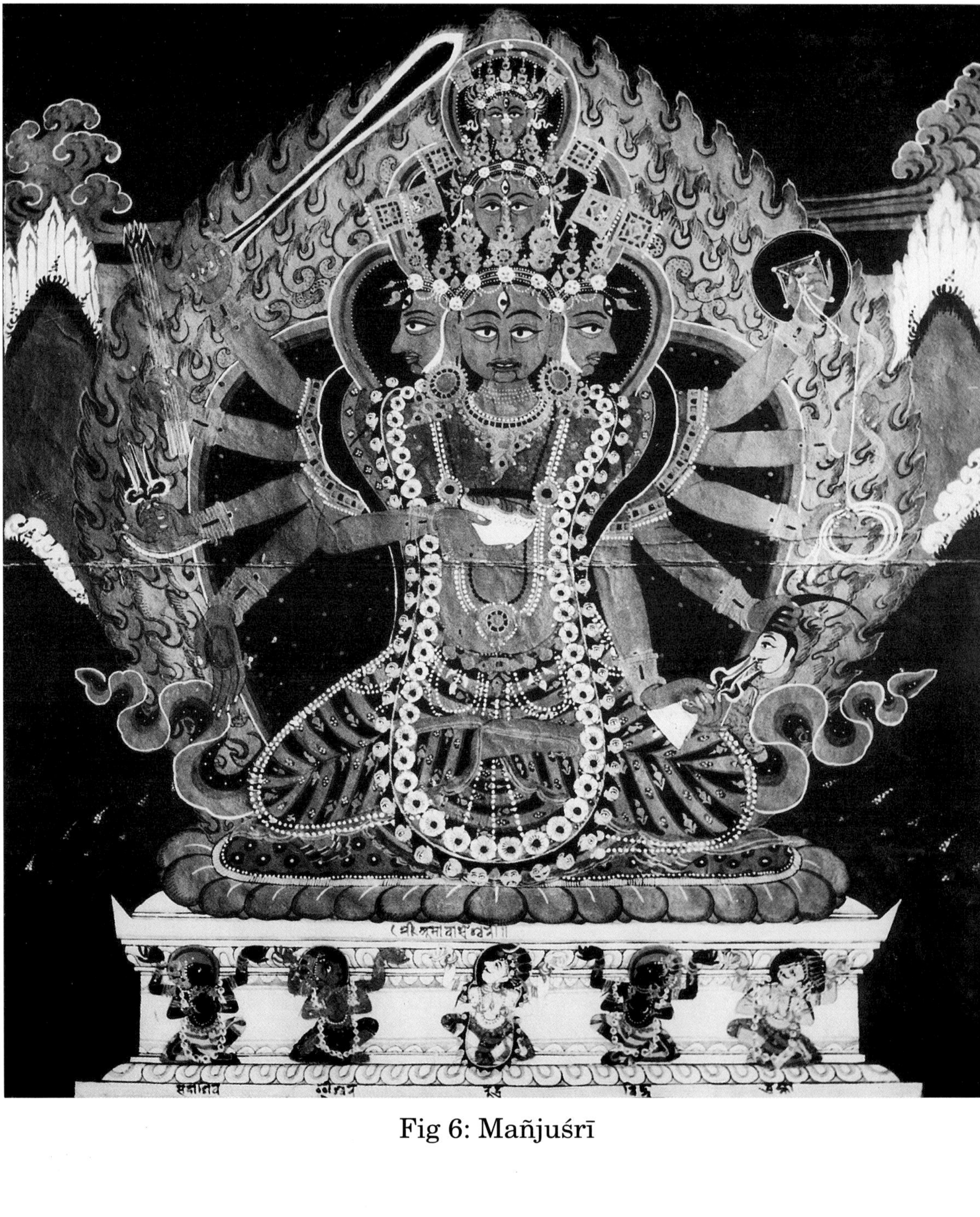

Fig 6: Mañjuśrī

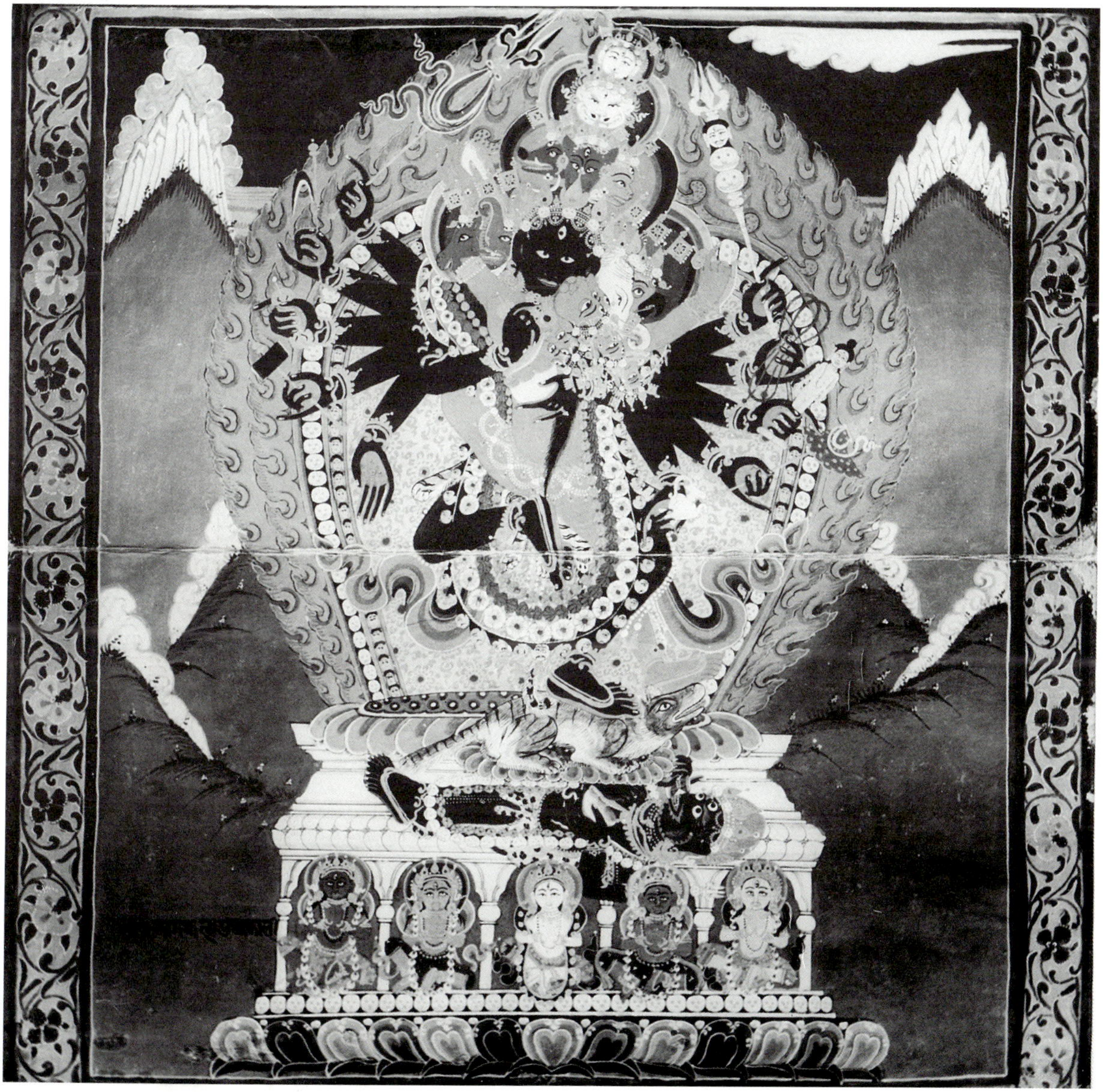

Fig 7: Heruka (Nairātmya)

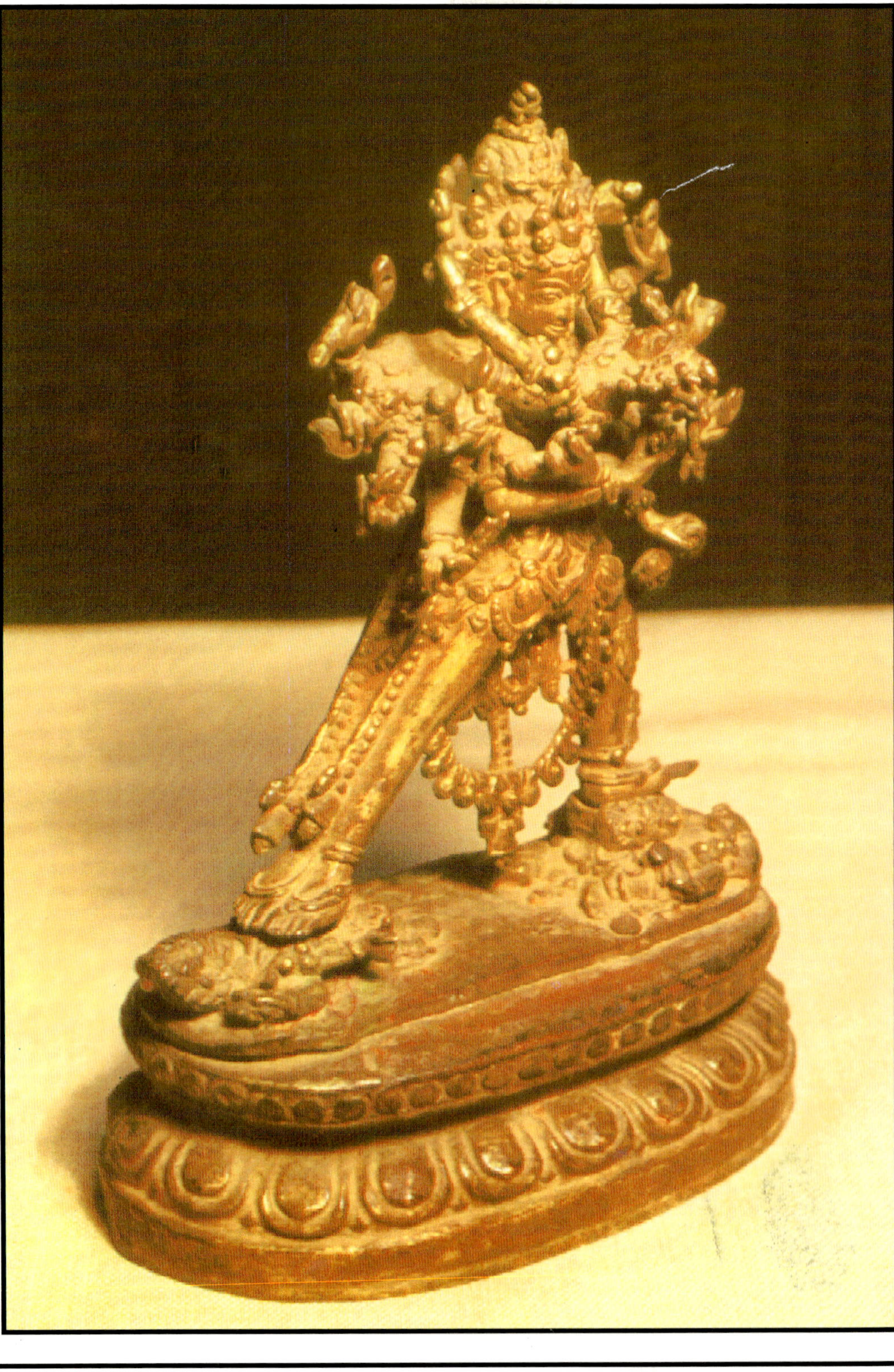

Fig 8: Hevajra (metal)

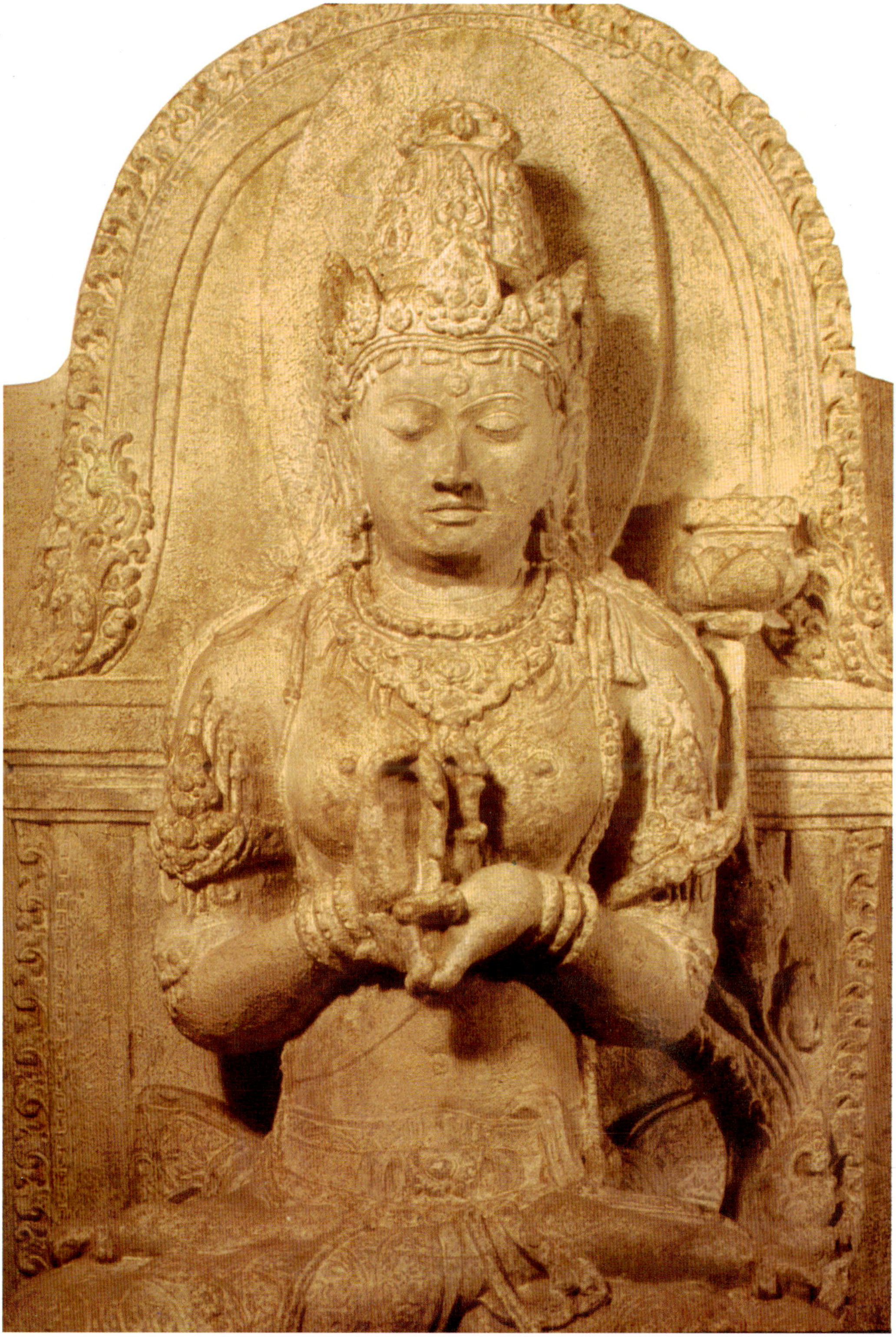

Fig 9: Prajñāpāramitā (stone)

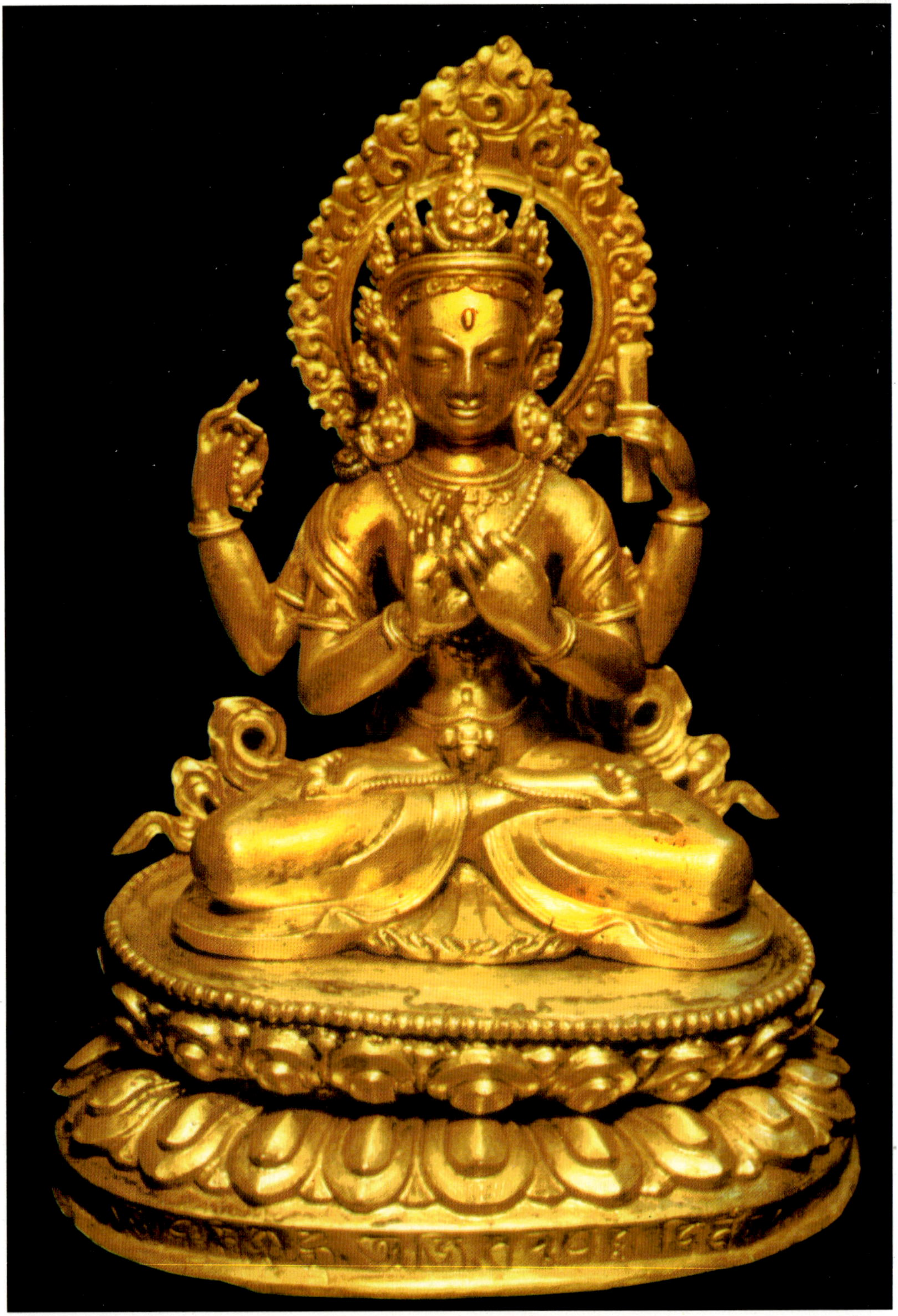

Fig 10: Prajñāpāramitā (metal)

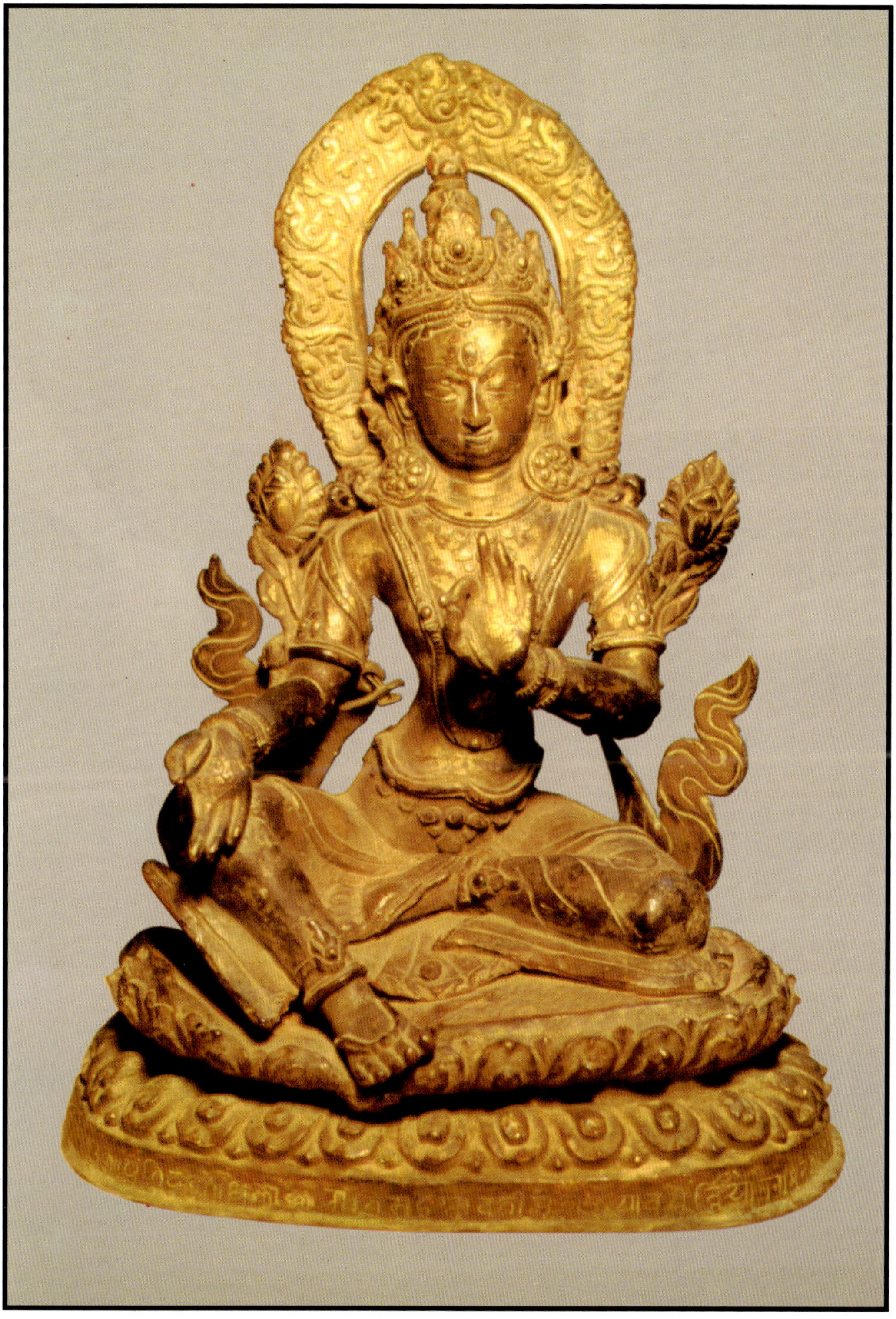

Fig 11: Tārā (metal)

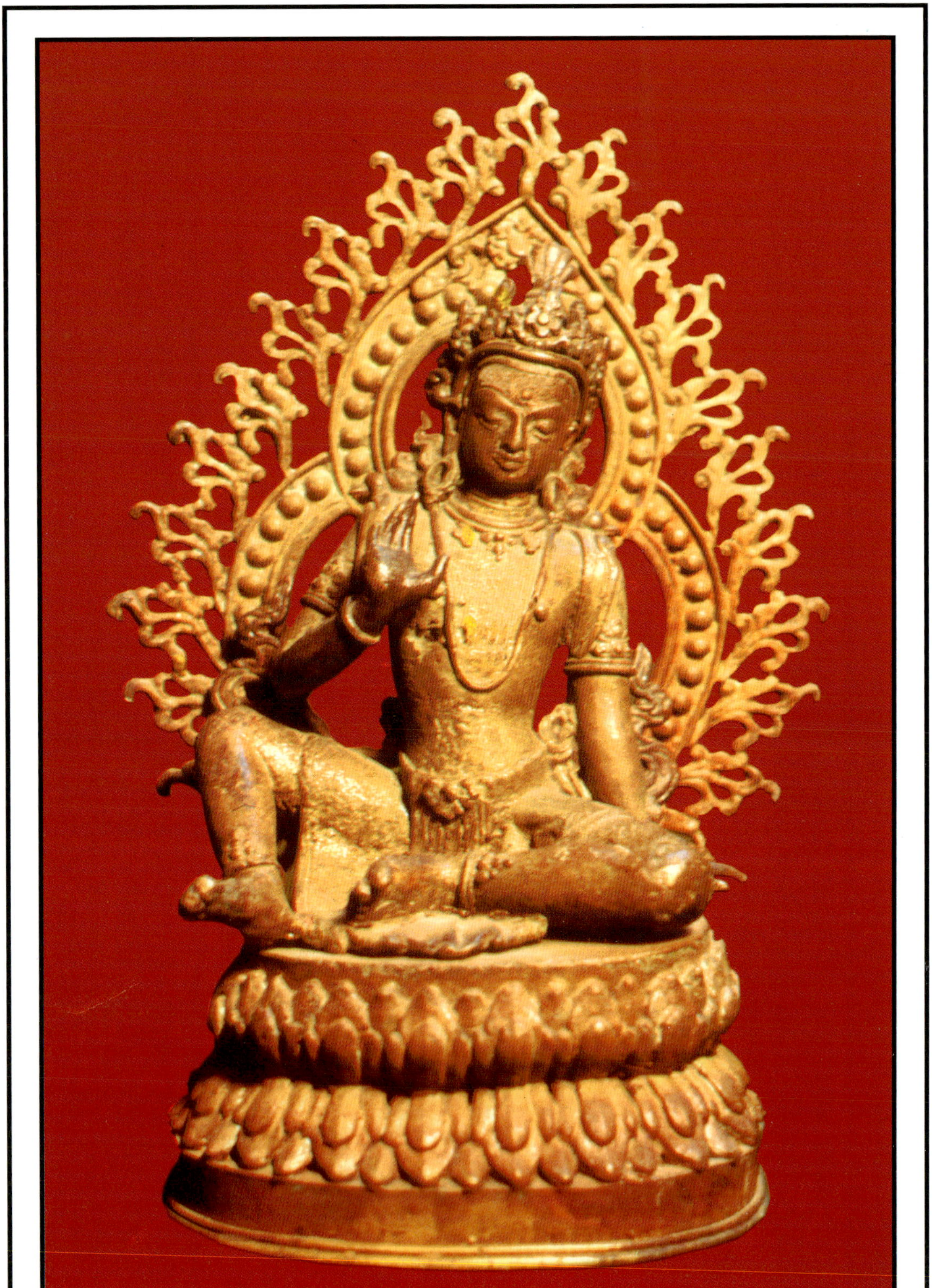

Fig 12: Avalokiteśvara (metal)

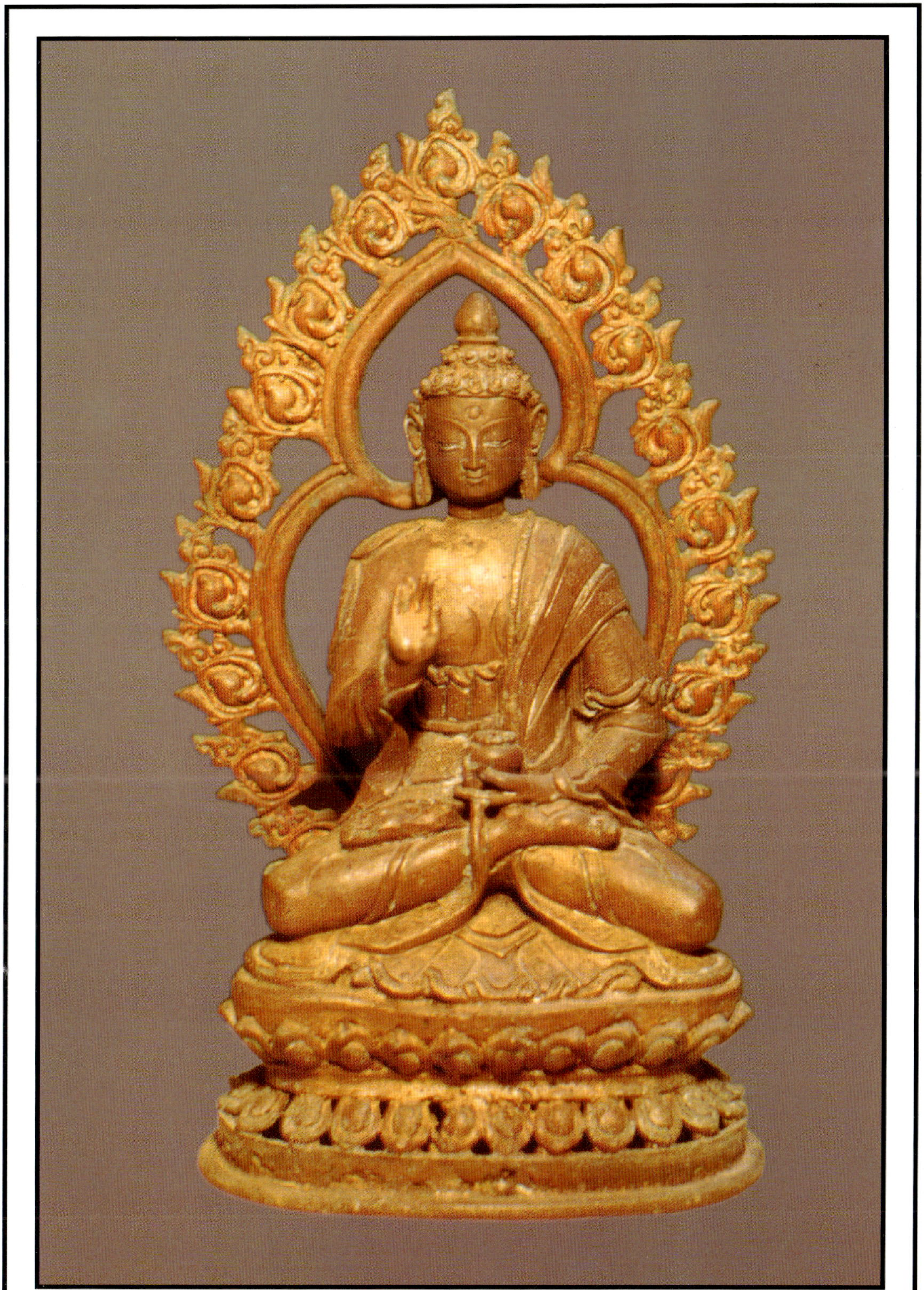

Fig 13: Amitāyuṣa (metal)

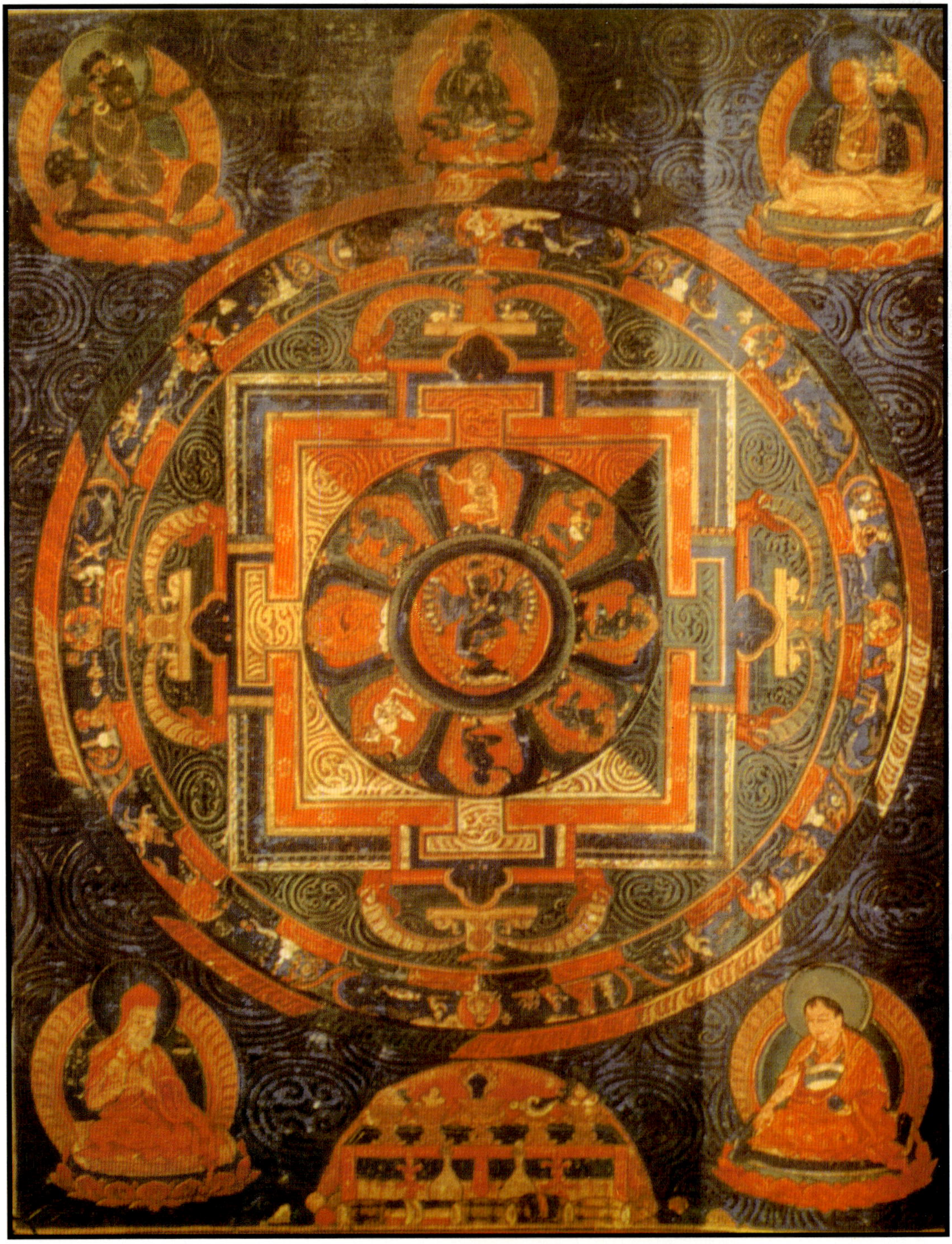

Fig 14: The maṇḍala of Heruka, Thangaka

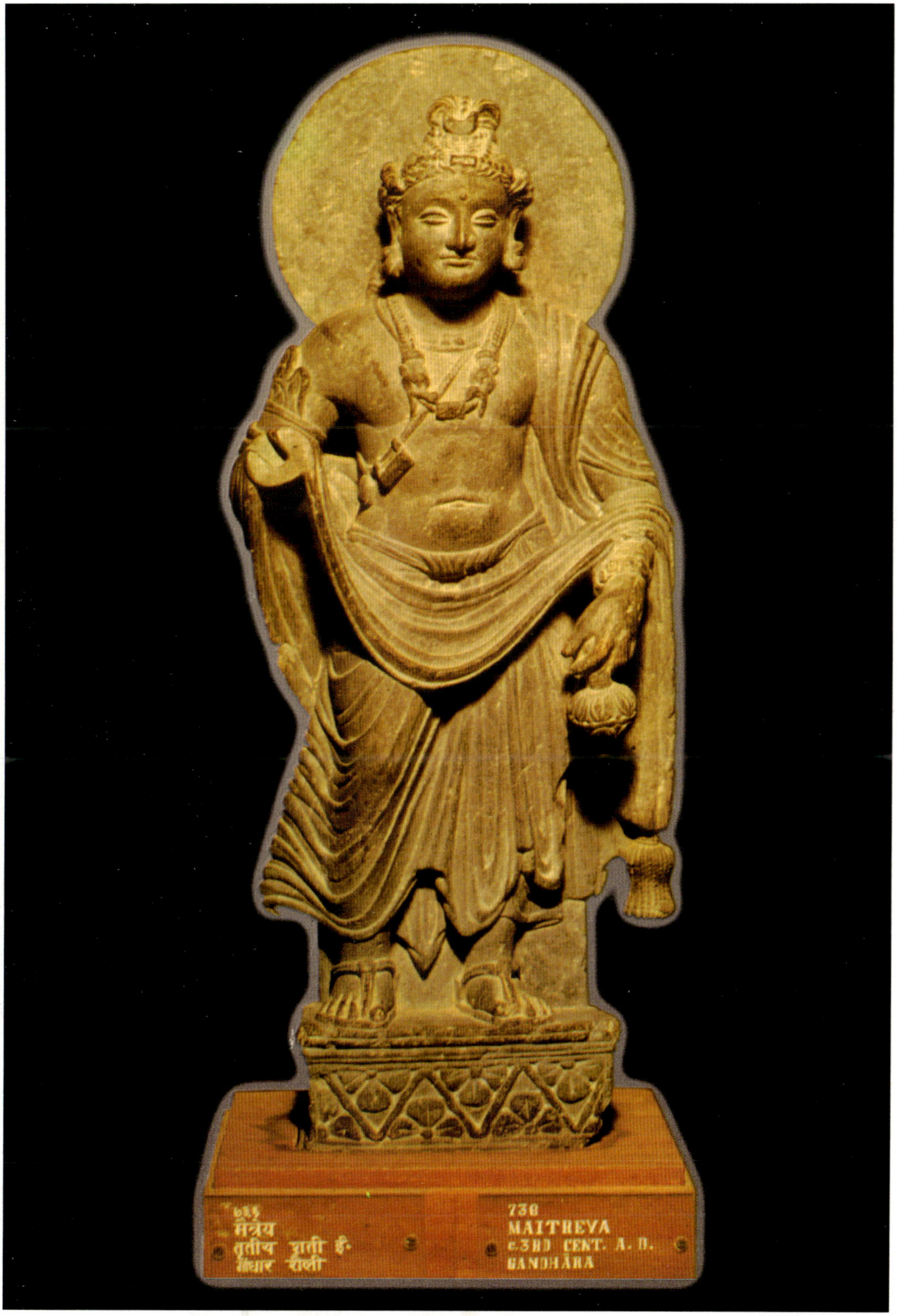

Fig 15: Bodhisattva

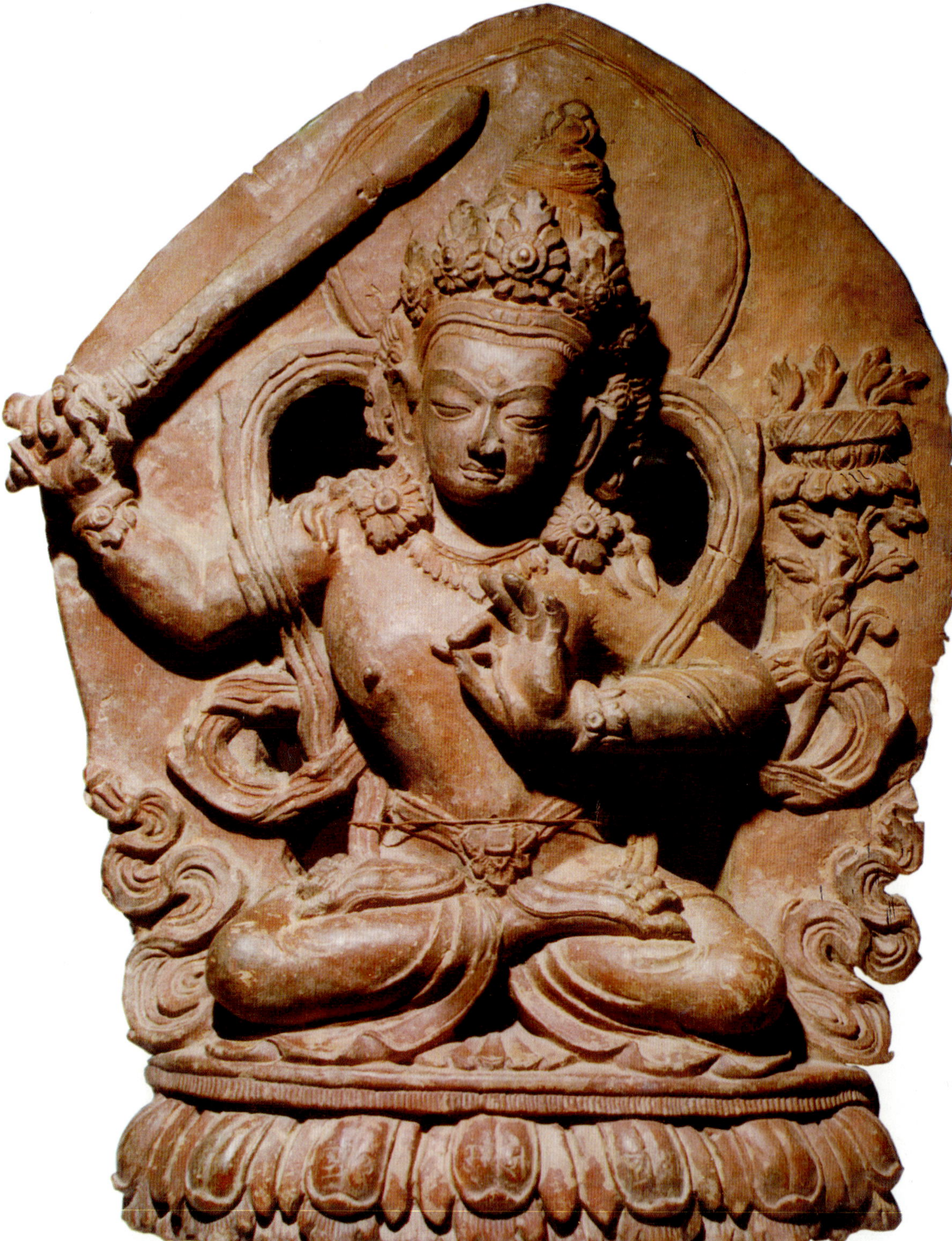

Fig 16: Mañjuśrī (teracotta)

Glossary

abhicāra	: Tāntric rituals.
ācāra	: Rule.
ādi	: Primal.
Ādi-Buddha	: Primordial Buddha.
Ādināth	: Primal Lord (Śiva).
advaya/advaita	: Non-dualism.
Aghora	: One of the five forms of Śiva.
agni	: Fire.
Akula	: The Śiva aspect of Śakti. According to Abhinavagupta, that which is manifested from *kula* or Śakti is Akula and it is endowed with the elements of Śiva.
amṛta	: Nectar, Embrosia.
anādi	: That which has no beginning.
anāhata	: One of the six nerve-plexuses (*ṣaṭcakra*) situated in the heart region. *Anāhata* is also the name of a particular form of sound.
ānanda	: Bliss; pleasure.
ānandamaya-kośa	: Sheath of bliss.

anātmatā : A term frequently used by Buddha without a clear definition. (Non-existence).

animā : The power of becoming as small as atom.

annamaya-kośa: Sheath of food.

aṇu : The term atom.

anugraha : Grace.

āp : Water.

aparā : The term for material or power knowledge.

arhat : An ideal person who is free from all worldly things.

arhat-hood : Liberated from cycle of birth and death.

āsana : Posture.

ātman : Self; the life principle.

ātmaśakti : Power of the Self.

avadhūta : The aspirant who commands universal reverence.

avadhūtikā : Avadhūtikā that is known as Suṣumnā nerve in the Hindu Tantra.

avidyā : Ignorance.

avyakta : The unmanifested. A synonym of *prakr̥ti* or primordial substance.

bam-bam : The mystic sound of Nāth *yogin*s.

bandha : Different kind of arrest.

bhaga : Female organ; vagina.

Bhagavatī : Goddess.

bhakti : Devotion.

bhāṇḍa : Body, pot.

bhāva : Disposition; state, mental certitude.

bhāvanā : A Pāli word, and it means culture or mental development.

bhoga : Enjoyment.

bhoktā : Eater.

bhūmi : Stages.

bhūta : Śiva; living being; the world; one of the five elements.

bhūtakoṭi : The end of existence.

Bhūtanātha : Śiva.

bīja : Seed, in Tantra it signifies the germ syllable which takes the form of a deity. It is also the term for semen.

bindu : Seed.

bodhi : Knowledge, wisdom.

bodhicitta : Blissful state of mind, enlightenment.

bodhimaṇḍala : Circle round the famous tree beneath which Buddha attain his bodhi.

bodhisattva : Attainment of wisdom, Buddha before enlightenment.

bodhisattva-hood : Who have reached the highest peak of bodhi.

brahmāṇḍa : Cosmos or cosmic egg.

Buddha : Perfectly enlightened one.

Buddhattva : Perfect enlightenment.

buddhi : Intelligence.

caitya : A sanctuary or shrine.

cakra : Circle, used in variety of *susa*s symbolising endless rotation of Śakti; cycle of the world process.

candra : Moon.

caryā : Observance.

cit : Intelligence or Consciousness.

cit-śakti : The principle of consciousness.

citta : Mind.

citta-bhūmi : The plane of mind.

citta-śuddhi : Purification of mind.

dakṣiṇa : It is the path of spiritual attainment without the use of *pañca-makāra* and other extreme forms of rituals.

deha : Body.

dhamma : Religion.

dharma : Religion.

dharma-dhātu : Totality of phenomenal manifestation, universal principal or universe.

dharma-kāya : Word of Buddha.

dhauti : Washing.

dhvani : Sound.

dhyāna : Meditation.

garimā : The power of becoming as heavy as one like.

grāhaka : Perceiver.

grāhya : Perceivable.

guhya : Secret.

guru : The preceptor or teacher who is the pivot in Tāntric *sādhanā*. *Guru* is one who dispels darkness.

haṭha-yoga : A form of physical exercise for making the body so disciplined as to serve for spiritual purposes. In *Haṭhayoga-pradīpikā*, 1.10, it is regarded as the source of all forms of *yoga*.

Hīnayāna : Lower vehicle, early Buddhism with emphasis on the doctrine, rather than on the worship of the Buddha.

icchā : Will.

icchā-śakti : Volition.

iḍā : One of the four principal nerves. As the symbol of moon, it is situated on the left side of the spinal cord.

iśitva : The power of obtaining supermacy over thing.

jāgrata : Wakefulness.

jīvana-mukti : Liberation with span of bodily existence, a very important Tāntric concept. He who has complete grasp of the knowledge of the self has dispelled from within the darkness of false knowledge by constant practice and meditation, and is reaping the fruits of his *karma*, may be called a *jīvana-mukti*.

jñāna : Knowledge; philosophical knowledge.

jñāna-śakti : Cognition.

jñāna-sattva : Attainment of wisdom, perfect wisdom.

kāla : Time; death and obstruction.

kāla-cakra : *Kāla-cakra* denoting wheel of time is the principal god of the Tāntric Buddhist Kālacakrayāna; wheel of destruction.

Kālacakrayāna : The vehicle for protection against the wheel of destruction.

kālāgni : The fire.

kālāgni : Destruction; fire of time.

kālī : Black.

kāma : Desire, passion.

kanyā : Girl.

kāraṇa : Tāntric term for wine.

kāraṇa-śarīra : Material body.

karma : Activity or action.

karuṇā : Universal compassion.

kaula : Non-duality.

kavaca : Amulets; armour, which saves the body from weapons.

kāyā : Body.

kleśa : Suffering.

kriyā : Action or activities.

kṣiti : Earth.

kula : Clan or family.

kulācāra : Family conduct.

*kulaśa*s : Lord of families.

kula-patha : The way through *kuṇḍalinī* pierces the *ṣaṭcakra*. Way of *kaula*.

kuṇḍalinī : The serpent power remaining latent in *mūlādhāra*.

kāya-sādhanā : Culture of body; the disciplining of the body.

laghimā : The power of assuming excessive lightness as will.

lalanā : The name of nerve, it is also known as the *āli* (left), and represents vowels.

liṅga : Male generative organ worshipped as a phallic symbol. *Liṅga* is the symbol of Śiva.

mahā : Great.

mahā-rāga : Intense emotion.

mahārajas : Ovum.

mahārasa : Great juice.

mahā-sattva : Attainment of wisdom.

mahāsukha : Great pleasure; bliss; blissful condition.

mahāsukha-sthāna : The place of great bliss.

Mahāyāna : Great vehicle; theistic form of Buddhism, with emphasis on divine Buddhas and *bodhisattvas*.

Maheśvara : Great Lord; Śiva.

mahimā : The power of becoming big.

maithuna : Sexual intercourse which is regarded as one of the five *makāras*. For spiritual interpretation see *Kulārṇva*, V., non-duality.

māṁsa : Flesh — one of the five *makāras*. It is supposed to be the body of Śiva.

manana : Logical thinking.

maṇḍala : A special gathering of aspirants for collective rituals of the five *makāras* where they sit in a circle (*cakra*) with their female partners; mystic circle.

maṇi : Male organ.

maṇipūra : A nerve (*cakra*) plexus near the naval region. It is also called *nābhīcakra*.

manomaya-kośa : Seath of lower mind.

mantra : Power (*śakti*) in the form of sounds, words, and letters. It (*mantra*) is ultimate reality in the form of sound; potency of sound.

mānuṣī Buddha : Human Buddha.

marut : Air.

matsya : Fish — which is one of the five *makāras*; symbolically, *matsya* is described as that which destroys the fetters and the bads to the path of salvation.

mokṣa : Salvation (*nirvāṇa*); please.

mudrā : *Mudrā* is also the name of one of the five *makāras*. In Buddhist Tantra, *mudrā* is used exclusively for the woman and her generative organ, posters gesture.

mukti : Salvation (*nirvāṇa*).

mūlādhāra : The first of the six nerve plexuses, it is situated in the lower extremity of the spinal cord where the *kuṇḍalinī* is coiled.

nāda : (a) Sound, (b) A term used in Tantra in a variety of senses. Its simple meaning is sound. In Tāntric concepts, the Supreme Being (*parā-śiva* or *parā-śakti*) is soundless and without any vibration. When this *parā-śakti* goes to express itself in creation, its first vibration is known as *nāda*. It is the manifestation of the consciousness of the Supreme Being revealed as sound. This manifestation is thought of in terms of the copulation of Śiva and Śakti (the static and kinetic aspects, also known as *prakāśa*, and *vimarśa*, of the same ultimate reality) and the thrill of the pleasure of this union (*maithuna*) is known as *nāda*.

nāda-brahma : *Nāda* concieve as *Brahman* in the form of primordial sound expressed in *parā*, *paśyantī*, *madhyamā*, and *vaikharī*.

nāḍī : Nerves of the human body; *pulśa*.

Nirañjana : Spickless.

nirātmā : Essencelessness.

nirguṇa : Attributeless.

nirmāṇa-kāya : Noumenal body.

nirvāṇa : Salvation; non-duality.

nivṛtti : Return current.

nyāsa : Identifying duties in different parts of the body of the devotee.

pada : Word.

padma : Lotus.

pañca-bhūta : Five material elements.

panth : Way; cult.

parā : Higher knowledge.

parabrahman : Supreme Being; the absolute; the ultimate reality in the form of pure consciousness.

paramānanda : Supreme bliss; realisation of full bliss.

paramasukha : Non-duality.

parā-mukti : Liberation.

parā-śabda : Motionless casual sound.

parā-śakti : *Parā-śakti* is the energy of Śiva which is regarded as the instrumental cause of creation. The term is also used to denote the power of independence of the Supreme Being. In the Śaiva and Śākta outlook, *parā-śakti* is the *vimarśa*, that is, vibrating or kinetic energy of the Supreme Being. It is equated with *kuṇḍalinī* and its functioning.

parā-vāk : It is the first stage of sound expressing itself only at *mūlādhāra*. It is without any vibration, it is like flame of light, unmanifested yet indestructible.

paśyantī : One of the constituents, it is regarded as the second stage of its development. This form of sound belongs to the naval region. It has little vibration and is connected with *nāda-tattva*.

piṇḍa : Body.

piṅgalā : One of the major nerves. Together with its sister nerve *iḍā* it rises from *mūlādhāra* and ends in the right nostril. It is also known as *sūrya-nāḍī* — having the masculine characteristics of the sun.

prajñā : Insight; knowledge; wisdom.

prakāmya : The power of obtaining all objects of pleasure at will.

prakṛti : Female principle of creation, variously conceived of as primordial matter or energy. Often identified with Śakti, the Supreme Being of the Śāktas; nature.

prāṇa/apāna : Vital wind; current.

prāṇāyāma : The process of breath control.

prāṇamaya-kośa : Sheath of life.

prāpti : The power of obtaining everything at will.

prasāda : Divine grace.

pravṛtti : Moving onward.

pṛthag-jana : Lay people.

pudgala : The non-existence of individuality (*ātman*) as also of the objective world (*dharma*).

pudgala-śūnyatā : Non-existence of any real substance as *ātman*.

pūjā : Worship.

puruṣa : Male principal of creation, later equated with the principles of sound and matter.

pūrva : Earlier.

rāga : Attachment; emotion.

rasa : Taste, sap, elixir, juice, sentiment. *Rasa* is also conceived in terms of intense emotional attachment between the male and female principles, symbolising two aspects of Śakti and impersonated by the aspirant and his partner.

rasanā : The name for nerve; it is also known as the *kālī* (right) which represents consonants.

rati : Sexual pleasure; the wife of *kāma*.

ṛddhi : Supernatural power.

rūpa : Form.

rūpa-kāya : Material element.

Saukhya : Pleasure.

sādhaka : Spiritual aspirant; seeker.

sādhanā : Term for spiritual exercise.

sahaja : (a) The way (*mārga*) of spiritual exercise which is the earliest and most natural. It is also the term for ultimate reality among the *sahajīyas*, i.e., those who believe in this *mārga*; (b) Non-duality, natural.

Sahajayāna : A section of Tāntric Buddhists which rose in revolt against Vajrayāna.

Śakti : Energy; female partner of the aspirant; it is the power of the Supreme Being conceived as the female principle through which the manifestation of the universe is effected. The important aspects of this power are *cit* (will), *jñāna* (knowledge), and *kriyā* (action).

sahasrāra : The highest cerebral region above; all the *cakras* or nerve-plexuses where *kuṇḍalinī* meets its source. For its description, see *Ṣaṭcakra-nirūpaṇa*, XLI-XLIII.

saṁbhoga-kāya : Body of bliss.

sambuddha : The perfectly enlightened one.

sāmantabhadra : Entirely auspicious.

sāmarasya : Equilibrium of Śiva and Śakti, male and female principles. In Buddhism it is that of *upāya* and *prajñā*. Very often this equilibrium is conceived of in sexual terms. Its spirit is felt by the aspirant within his own self. Complete understanding of this equilibrium leads to the experience of non-duality.

samādhi : State of perfect bliss in which the world of senses disappears from the mind of the aspirant. It is the aim of all yogic exercises — non-duality.

saṁjñā : Name or conceptual knowledge; perception.

saṁsāra : World.

saṁskāra : Mental state; impression.

samyak-sambuddha : Perfect enlightened one.

samarasa : The state of unity of emotion or oneness of emotion.

sat : Existence.

ṣaṭcakra : The six nerve-plexuses, i.e., *mūlādhāra*, *svādhiṣṭhāna*, *maṇipūra*, *anāhata*, *viśuddha*, and *ājñā*.

stūpa : Buddhist relic mound.

siddha/siddhi : *Siddhi* is spiritual attainment. The term is also used to denote the attainment of miraculous power. He or she who has attained *siddhi* is known as *siddha*.

śiṣya : Disciple.

śukra : Semen.

śukram/vīrya : Semen.

sukha : Bliss.

sukhāvatī : The seat of all happiness; the abode of bliss.

sukha-maya : Incessant bliss.

summum-bonum : This is known as Mahāsukha.

suṣupta/suṣupti : Deep sleep.

śūnya : Reality, Void.

Śūnyavāda : Nihilism.

śunyatā : Attributeless; vacuity, pure void; perfect knowledge. The Buddhist idea of vacuity conceived of in terms of the female principle. It is also known as *prajñā*, and symbolised in the form of different goddess. The male principle is thought of as *karuṇā* and *upāya*.

sūrya : Sun.

suṣumnā : The most important nerve, also known as *brahma-nāḍī*. It is said that universe itself is contained in this nerve. It extends from the *mūlādhāra* to *brahma-randhra*. It is the route by which *kuṇḍalinī* marches upwards.

sahajānanda : Non-duality; more intense bliss or perfect bliss.

skanda : Elements.

svapna : Illusion; dream.

śrāvaka : Buddhist monk.

spanda : Motion.

sparśa : Touch.

sthāna : Place.

soma : A drink; a plant; the elixir of immortality.

svādhiṣṭhāna : The nerve-plexus situated above the *mūlādhāra*.

tanmātra : Potential elements.

tattva : Essential principles.

tejas : Fire; Fiery energy.

tri-dhātu : Three elements.

trikoṇa : Triangle, also known as *yoni*; female generative organ.

turīya : A very high state. The *sahasrāra-cakra* is supposed to contain a field of knowledge which is also known as *turīya*.

ulṭā-sādhanā : Regressive process.

upabhogya : Food.

upāya : Method or means.

upāsanā : Worship.

uttara : Later.

vibhūti : Supernatural power.

vācaka/vācya : *Śakti* or power of *mantra*: the former the denoting or signifying aspect; while the latter is the basic one. *Vācya* is contained in the *vācaka* and formally there is no distinction between them.

vāhana : Vehicle.

vāk : Speech.

Vajrayāna : A form of Tāntric Buddhism.

vajra : Thunderbolt.

vajra-kāya : Adament vehicle.

vāyu : Wind.

vaśitva : The power of subduing, fascinating, or bewitching.

viśuddha : The nerve plexus above the *anāhata* in the neck.

vicitra : The moment when the realisation of pleasure is resulting from physical union (*ānanda*).

vihāra : Monastery.

vijñāna : Ego-consciousness/consciousness.

vijñānamaya-kośa : Sheath of higher mind.

vilakṣaṇa : The realisation of bliss is free from any emotion of attachment or detachment (*sahajānanda*).

vimarda : When realisation of bliss is attended with the consciousness of the ego as the realiser of the bliss (*virāmānanda*).

vindu : A term used in a variety of senses. As a dot denotes Śiva and as a double dot (*visarga*), Śakti, both being alphabetical signs. The former stands for solar power, the latter for lunar. In Śaiva conception, *vindu* is an evolute of *nāda* which is produced owing to the *kriyā-śakti* of Śiva. It also stands for the male organ while *visarga* denotes the female organ.

vipāka : A kind of mental state when the bliss is matured to knowledge (*paramānanda*).

virāmānanda : Detachment from the worldly pleasure.

visarga : Alphabetical sign of double dot which is symbolically regarded as the complementary *śakti* of *vindu*. It signifies both the *parā* and *aparā* aspects of Śakti. It is the female principle (*sah*) as complementary to the male principle (*ham*).

vyakta : Manifest or form.

vyavadhāna : Distinction.

vedanā : Feeling; sensation.

vyoma : Ether.

yantra : Symbol of deity. It is generally the form of diagram or geometrical pattern serving as a chart for revealing the characteristics of the deity.

yān : Way (Paths).

yāmala : Non-duality.

yoga : Disciplining of the body for various purposes — physical, mental, and spiritual and meditation.

yogācāra : One who practises *yoga*.

yoni : Female generative organ.

yugal : Non-duality.

yuganaddha : Male principle in union with the female principle. It is the non-dual state of unity of *śūnyatā* and *karuṇā*.

yuvatī : Young woman.

Bibliography

Abhinavaguptacharya, *Śrī Tantra Loka*, Part IV, Srinagar, Govt. Publication, 1922.

Acharya, Narendra Deo, *Bouddha Dharma Darśana*, Patna, 1956.

Agrawal, Vasudeo Sarana, *Harṣacarita, Ek Sānskṛtik Adhyayana* (in Hindi), Patna, 1964.

———, *Śiva-Mahadeo*, Patna, 1966.

Allchin, Bridget, and Raymond, *The Birth of Indian Civilisation,* Great Britain, 1968.

Anand, Mulk Raj, and Lance Dane, *Kāma-Sūtra of Vātsyāyana*, New Delhi, 1982.

———, *Kāma-Kalā*, New York, 1958.

Apte, Vamana Shivrama, *Sanskrit-Hindi Kośa*, Varanasi, 1966.

Aśvaghoṣa, *Buddhacarita*, tr. E.H., Johnston, Reprint, Delhi, 1972.

Bagachi, P.C., *Studies in the Tantras*, Part I, Calcutta, 1939.

———, *Pre-Dravidian and Pre-Aryan in India*, Calcutta, 1929.

———, *Kaulajñānanirṇaya and Some Minor Texts of the School of Matsyendranath*, Calcutta, 1934.

Banerjea, J.N., *The Development of Hindu Icnography*, Calcutta, 1956.

———, *Paurāṇic and Tāntric Religion*, Calcutta, 1966.

Barua, B.M., *Pre-Buddhistic Indian Philosophy*, reprint, Delhi, 1970.

Basham, A.L., *A Cultural History of India*, London, 1975.

Basu, Manoranjan, *Tantra, A General Study*, Calcutta, 1976.

Benjamin Rowland Jr., *The Evolution of The Buddha Image*, New York, 1963.

Bhandarkar, R.G., *Vaiṣṇavism, Śaivism, and other Minor Religious Systems*, reprint, Varanasi, 1965.

Bharati, *Bulletin of the College of Indology,* Banaras Hindu University, No. 3, 1959-60, Varanasi.

Bharati, Agehananda, *Tāntric Tradition*, New Delhi, 1983.

Bharati, Dharmavir, *Siddha-Sāhitya* (in Hindi), Allahabad, 1950.

Bhattacharya, B.T., *An Introduction to the Buddhist Esoterism*, London, 1932.

———, *Indian Buddhist Iconography*, Calcutta, 1959.

Bhattacharyya, Dipak Chandra, *Tāntric Buddhist Iconographic Sources*, New Delhi, 1973.

———, *Studies in Buddhist Iconography*, New Delhi, 1978.

Bhattacharya, H.N., *The Indian Mother Goddess*, New Delhi, 1977.

———, *The History of Śākta Religion*, Delhi, 1974.

———, *Ancient Indian Rituals*, New Delhi, 1975.

———, *The History of the Tāntric Religion*, New Delhi, 1982.

———, *The History of Indian Erotic Literature*, New Delhi, 1975.

———, *Tāntric Buddhism*, New Delhi, 1999.

Bhattacharya, Tarapada, *The Canons of Indian Art*, Calcutta, 1963.

Bhattasali, H.K., *Iconography of Buddhist and Brāhmaṇical Sculptures in the Dacca Museum*, Dacca, 1929.

Bose, D.N. and Hira Lal, Haldhar, *Tantra: Their Philosophy and Occult Secrets*, Calcutta, 1981.

Bramha, Nalani Kant, *Philosophy of Hindu Sādhanā*, London, 1932.

Briggs, G.W., *Gorakha Nātha and the Kanphaṭa Yogīs*, Calcutta, 1938.

Chakravarti, C., *Tantras, Studies on their Religion and Literature*, Calcutta, 1963.

Chatterjee, S.C. and D.M., Datta, *An Introduction to Indian Philosophy*, Calcutta, 1939.

Chaturvedi, Sita Ram, *Kālidāsa Granthāvalī* (Sanskrit-Hindi), Varanasi, 1980.

Coomaraswamy, Anand K., *The Origin of the Buddha Image*, New Delhi, 1972.

———, *Elements of Buddhist Iconography*, London, 1935.

———, *Cultural Heritage of India*, Vol. I-V, Calcutta.

Dasgupta, S.B., *An Introduction to Tāntric Buddhism*, Calcutta, 1974.

———, *Aspects of Indian Religious Thought*, Calcutta, 1957.

———, *Obscure Religious Cults*, 2nd edn., Calcutta, 1962.

Datta, R.C., *Pracīn Bhārat Kī Sabhyatā Kā Itihāsa* (in Hindi), Allahabad, 1966.

De, Sushil Kumar, *Ancient Indian Erotics and Erotic Literature*, Calcutta, 1959.

Desai, Devangana, *Erotic Sculpture of India: A Socio-Cultural Study*, New Delhi, 1975.

Deussen, Paul, *The Philosophy of the Upaniṣad*, reprint, New Delhi, 1979.

Dwivedi, Hazari Prasad, *Nāth Sampradāya* (in Hindi), Allahabad, 1959.

Eggeling, J., *Śatapatha Brāhmaṇa*, 1963.

George, Christopher, *The Candamaharasana Tantra*, New Haven, 1974.

Gordon, D.H., *Pre-Historic Background of Indian Culture*, Bombay, 1958.

Gosh, Aurobindo, *The Synthesis of Yoga*, Arya, 1918.

Guenther, H.V., *Yuganaddha, The Tāntric View of Life*, 2nd edn., Banaras, 1964.

Gupta, Sanjukta, *Prapanchsar*, Leiden, 1972.

———, *History and Culture of Indian People*, Vol. I-X, Bombay.

———, *The Age of Imperial Kanauj*, Vol. IV, Bombay.

———, *Indian Archaeology — A Review*, 1958-9, 1962-3.

———, *Indian Historical Quarterly*, March, 1933.

John Woodroffe, *Principles of Tantra*, Madras, 1952.

Joshi, Lalmani, *Studies in Buddhist Culture of India*, Banaras, 1967.

Joshi, Pandit Harishankar, *Vedic Viśvadarśan*, Banaras Hindu University, Varanasi, 1966.

Kalyana (Sivanka), *Samvat*, 1990; *Kalyana* (Saktyank), 1991, Gita Press, Gorakhpur, 1991.

Kane, P.V., *History of Dharmaśāstra*, 5 Vols., Poona, 1962.

Kaviraj, Gopinath, *Journal of Ganga Nath Jha Research Institute*, Vol. III, Allahabad.

———, *Tāntric Sāhitya* (in Hindi), Lucknow, 1972.

———, *Gopinath Kaviraj Abhinandan Grantha*, Lucknow, 1967.

———, *Bhāratīya Sanskṛti aur Sādhanā*, Part I & II (in Hindi), Patna, 1963 and 1964.

———, *Tāntric Vāṅgamaya aur Śākta Dṛṣṭi* (in Hindī), Patna, 1963.

Kazi, Dawa Samdup, *Cakrasambhavatantra*, Calcutta, 1919.

Keith, A.B., *The Religion and Philosophy of Veda and Upaniṣad*, Varanasi, 1965.

———, *Taittirīya Saṁhitā*, Varanasi, 1967.

———, *Ṛgveda Brāhmaṇas, and Aitareya and Kauṣītaki Brāhmaṇas of the Ṛgveda*, 1920.

———, *The Karma Mīmāṁsā*, London, 1921.

Kern, H., *Manual of Indian Buddhism*, Strassbour, 1996.

Kosambi, D.D., *Myth and Reality*, Bombay, 1962.

———, *The Culture and Civilisation of Ancient India*, New Delhi, 1962.

Lokesh Chandra, *The Thousand Armed Avalokiteśvara*, New Delhi, 1988.

Lorenzen, D.H., *The Kāpālikas and Kālāmukhas* (To Lost Śaivite Sects), New Delhi, 1972.

Mallick, Kalyani, *Nāthasampradāya Itihās Darśana O Sādhanā-praṇālī* (in Bengali), Calcutta, 1950.

Marshall, J., *Mohenjo-daro and Indus Civilisation*, London, 1930.

———, *Buddhist Art of Gāndhāra*, London, 1961.

Max-Müllar, *The Upaniṣad*, Delhi, 1965.

Mishra, Ram Prasad, *Sahajayāna*, Calcutta, 1991.

Mishra, T.N., *Bhāratīya Prācya Sāhitya Mẽ Śiva kā Svarūpa*, "Pariṣad Patrika", Verse 25, Ank 3, Patna, 1985.

———, *Impact of Tantra on Religion and Art*, New Delhi, 1997.

Mitra, Debala, *Buddhist Monuments*, Calcutta, 1971.

Mookerjee, Ajit, *Tantra Asana*, New Delhi, 1971.

———, *Tantra Art*, New Delhi, 1971.

Mookerjee, Ajit and Madhu Khanna, *The Tāntric Way*, London, 1977.

Novonemes, M.M., *Gopinath Kaviraj Smṛti Granth* (in Hindi), Varanasi, 1987.

Pant, Ramesha Chandra, *Early Hindu Civilisation*, Calcutta, 1963.

Pathak, V.S., *The History of Śaiva Cults in Northern India*, Varanasi, 1960.

Pusalkar, A.D., *Studies in the Epics and Purāṇas*, Bombay, 1955.

Radhakrishnan, S., *Principal Upaniṣads*, London, 1953.

———, *The Hindu View of Life*, London, 1957.

———, *The Brahma Sūtra: The Philosophy of Spiritual Life*, London, 1960.

———, *History of Philosophy: Eastern and Western*, London, 1952.

———, *The Dammapada*, Oxford, 1950.

Randhawa, M.S., *The Cult of Trees and Tree-Worship in Buddhist-Hindu Sculpture*, New Delhi, 1964.

Rao, T.A. Gopinath, *Elements of Hindu Iconography*, Vol. I & II, Madras.

Ray, Niharranjan, *Idea and Image in Indian Art*, New Delhi, 1973.

Rockhill, W.W., *The Life of Buddha*, reprint, Varanasi, 1972.

Saraswati, S.K., *Tantrayāna Art — An album*, Calcutta, 1977.

Sastri, Hari Prasad, *Advaya Saṁgraha*, Gayakwad Oriental Series, Baroda, 1927.

Sastri, Gopal, *Manu-smṛti*, Varanasi, 1982.

———, *Manu-smṛti or Law of Manu*, tr. G. Bühler, S.B.E., Vol. XXV, 1964.

Shastri, Mahadeva, *Brahma Sūtra* (Śankara Bhāṣya), 1915.

Sastri, Manamatha Nath, *Agni Purāṇa*, Varanasi, 1967.

Sastri, Ram Sen, *Devī Bhāgavata*, Varanasi, 1965.

Satavalakar, Sripada Damodar, *Mahābhārata*, Parodi.

Sharma, L.N., *Kaśmīr Śaivism*, Varanasi, 1972.

Sharma, Neela Kamal, *Prācīn Bhārata Mē Śakti Pūjā* (in Hindi), Poona, 1986.

Sharma, Shiva Dutta, *Nirukta*, 1904.

Sharma, R.S., *Aspects of Political Ideas and Institutions in Ancient India*, New Delhi, 1959.

———, *Indian Feudalism: 300-1200*, Calcutta, 1965.

Sharma, Ram Swarupa Z., *Śvetāśvatara Upaniṣad*, Bombay, 1913.

Sinha, B.C., *Hinduism and Symbol Worship*, Delhi, 1983.

Simha, Amar, *Amarakośa*, Chowkhamba Sanskrit Series, Varanasi, 1970.

Singh, Bhagawati Prasad, *Manisi kī Lokayātra* (in Hindi), Varanasi, 1980.

Singh, Ram Dular, ed., *Aghora Granthāvali* (in Hindi), 1986.

Snellgrove, D.L., *Buddhist Himālayas*, Oxford, 1957.

———, ed., *The Image of Buddha*, New Delhi, 1978.

Srinivasachari, P.N., *Advaita and Viśiṣṭādvaita*, Bombay, 1961.

Tatia, N., *Studies in Jaina Philosophy*, Bombay, 1951.

Upadhyaya, Baldev, *Bhāratīya Darśana* (in Hindi), Varanasi, 1966.

———, *Bouddha Darśana Mīmāṁsā*, Varanasi, 1954.

Upadhyay, Ganga Prasad, *Advaitavāda*, Allahabad.

Upadhyay, Nagendra Nath, *Tāntric Bouddha Sādhanā aur Sāhitya* (in Hindi), Kasi, Samvat, 2015 (1958).

———, *Bouddha Kāpālika Sādhanā aur Sāhitya* (in Hindi), Allahabad, 1983.

Wayman, Alex, *Female Energy and Symbolism in the Buddhist Tantra, History of Religion*, Vol. II, No. 1, 1962.

———, *"Buddhism", in Historia Religion*, ed. C. Jouco Bluker and Geo Widengren, Vol. 2, Laiden, 1971.

———, *Yoga of the Guhyasamaja-tantra*, Delhi, 1977.

William, M., *A Sanskrit-English, Dictionary*, London, 1956.

Williams, R., *Jaina Yoga*, London, 1963.

Winternitz, M., *History of Sanskrit Literature*, 3 Vol. Delhi, 1972.

Woodroffe, J., *The Serpent Power, being the Ṣaṭcakra Nirūpaṇa*, Madras, 1958.

Zimmer, H., *The Art of India Asia*, New York, 1955.

———, *Myths and Symbols in Indian Art and Civilisation*, U.S.A., 1963.

Advayavajra Saṁgraha

Atharvaveda (in Hindi), ed. Satavasakar, Parodi, 1989.

Bhagavat Gītā, Gorakhpur, Samvat, 2040.

Bṛhadāraṇyaka Upaniṣad, Varanasi, 1983.

Chāndogya Upaniṣad, Gita Press, Gorakhpur, Samvat, 2013.

Devī Bhāgavata, Ram, Sastri; Taj; Varanasi, 1965.

Gorakṣa-Saṁhitā.

Guhyasamāja-tantra, Gaekwad Oriental Series, No. 53, Baroda, 1967.

Haṭhayoga-Pradīpika, tr. Pancham Singh, Allahabad, 1955.

Hevajra Tantra, ed. and tr. D.L. Snellgrove, London, 1959.

Jaiminīya Brāhmaṇa.

Jñānārṇava Tantra, ed. G.S. Goknati, Poona, 1952.

Jñānasiddhi, G.O.S. No. XLIV, 57.

Kālacakra-tantra: Exposition of Dalai Lama, XIV, ed. Jeffery Hopkins, Dharamasala, 1985.

Kaṭhopaniṣad, Varanasi, 1983.

Kaula-Jñāna-Nirṇaya.

Kauṣītaki Brāhmaṇa.

Kena Upaniṣad, Varanasi, 1983.

Kulāraṇava Tantra, Tāntric Text, Vol. V, London, 1917.

Māṇḍūkyopaniṣad, Gita Press, Gorakhpur.

Mantra Mahodadhi.

Muṇḍaka Upaniṣad, ed. Vidya Nand Giri, Risikesh, 1978.

Niṣpannayogāvali, ed. B. Bhattacharyya, Gaekwads' Oriental Series, No. CIX, Baroda, 1949.

Paraśurāma Kalpa Sūtra, Gaekwad's Oriental Series, Vols. XXII-XXIII.

Ṛgveda (in Hindi), ed. Satavalekar, Parodi, 1983.

Rudra Yāmala, Calcutta, 1937.

Śakti Saṅgam, G.O.S. Nos. LXI, CIV, Baroda, 1932-47.

Śāradātilaka, Tāntric Texts, Vols. XVI, XVII, Calcutta, 1933.

Saundarya Laharī, ed. A. Kuppuswami, New Delhi, 1991.

Śivamahimna Strotram (Puspadanta), Varanasi, 1964.

Śrī-Kālacakra-tantra.

Śrī Tattva-Cintāmaṇi.

Taittirīya Upaniṣad, Gita Press, Gorakhpur.

Sacred Book of the East: *The Vedānta Sūtras*, Vol. 34, 38 (in 2 vols.) with commentary by Śaṅkarācārya.

———, *The Vedānta-Sūtras with Rāmānuja Śrībhāṣya*, Vol. XLVIII (48), Delhi.

Sacred Book of the Hindus, ed. B.D. Basu.

Sādhanamāla, Gaekwad's Oriental Series, No. 26, 41, Baroda, 1968.

Standard English-Hindi Dictionary, 2nd ed., Allahabad, 1983.

Index